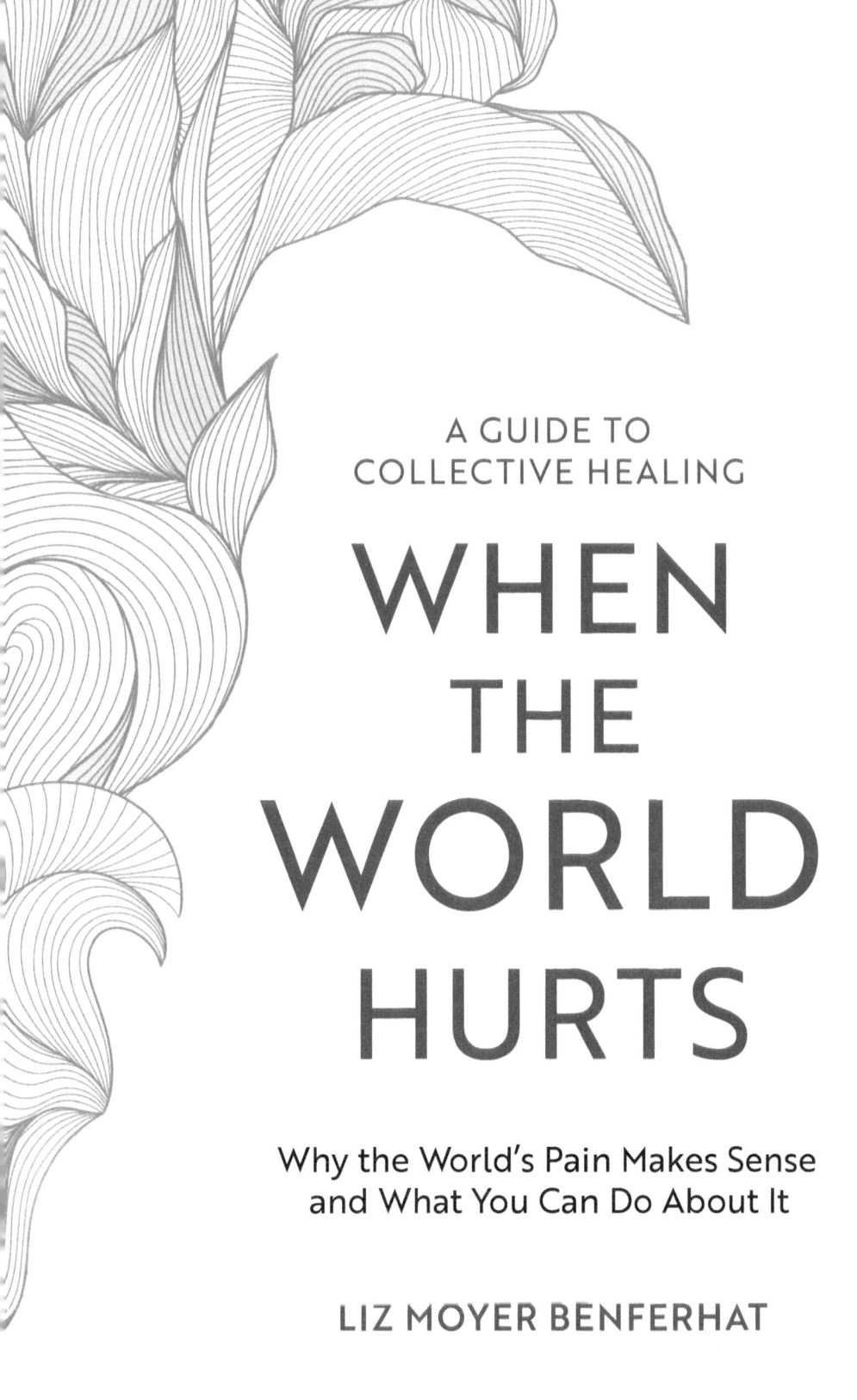

A GUIDE TO
COLLECTIVE HEALING

WHEN
THE
WORLD
HURTS

Why the World's Pain Makes Sense
and What You Can Do About It

LIZ MOYER BENFERHAT

*To We Heal For All, as a soul and spiritual essence
who's been calling me to bring her forth
and share her with the world.*

Thanks for choosing me.

To my family, friends, and creative partners,
from the bottom of my heart—
thank you
for the energy and prayers you put into this.

I couldn't have done it without you.

AUTHOR'S NOTE

I wrote this book from 2018 to 2025, with the heart of the writing taking place from 2023 to 2025. Current events, stories, and references reflect that. I also write this as an American, therefore stories and examples are primarily sourced from the US context, though I hope they resonate more broadly.

"Nothing that feels bad is ever the last step."
EUGENE GENDLIN

TABLE OF CONTENTS

PART I

WHERE WE BEGIN

Chapter 1:

AN INVITATION

Welcome to this book and our shared space.

It might sound like an odd way to phrase it, but as I've gone about writing this book, I've thought about it as a shared space between you and me and all of the other hearts and souls who choose to read it. In this way, it's like a workshop—or an experience. But "experience" feels a little too airy-fairy for me, so let's just stick with workshop.

In the pages that follow, it's my hope that this workshop-of-a-book will help you form a healthier relationship with our world—a world that's changing fast and in a lot of pain—and that, I believe, is ripe for transformation.

If you've ever...

If you've ever scrolled through the news and felt the world's pain punch you in your gut and drop you to your knees... If you've found yourself lying awake at three in the morning, with your mind spinning about the latest political crisis or climate report, wondering what to do about it all... If you're tired of feeling like you have to choose between caring deeply and protecting your sanity...

If you've watched political fights tear friend groups apart... If you've found yourself avoiding certain relatives because every conversation becomes a battlefield… If you're exhausted by political extremes, feeling like neither side represents your values…

If you're trying to live your values without being preachy or performative… If you're trying to raise kids while navigating a world that's upside down… If you just want to be a good person but can't figure out what that looks like anymore…

Welcome. You've found your people.

As I look around right now, especially in my home country of the United States, it's no secret that we as a collective are going through a lot. Society's pain is up in our faces in a way it never has been before. From social media doom scrolling to a 24/7 news cycle that won't quit, we are inundated with information about the big issues we're up against, and the consensus headline is, "We're fucked." From the climate crisis to war to mass incarceration to school shootings to rapid species loss, artificial intelligence, political breakdown, media bias, corporate greed… the list goes on. (*I'm panting and sweating*). The world is in serious pain, and we're feeling it.

Whether you pay attention to things at the global or the local level; topics related to technology or the Earth; issues that are "red" or "blue," there is a whole host of very big and very normal feelings that come with being alive and attuned to the changes in our world. From overwhelm, existential dread, utter indignation, and deep heartache… to wonder, excitement, and awe. Being in relationship with the world requires us to be in relationship with complicated feelings that match the complexity of our times.

You're not alone (and this all makes sense)

Many of us are opting out from it all. Squeezing our eyes tight, holding our breath, waiting for all of this to be over. The dysfunction and harshness are too much to handle. Others of us can't look away. It's like watching a train wreck! We laugh and munch on popcorn in a dissociated state that makes it bearable to engage with. Then there are others of us who are taking it all on and breaking down: sleepless nights, knots in our stomachs. We must act now! Wheels are spinning, but is progress being made?

As a changemaker and self-identified feeler, I can relate to all of these responses. It's why I went into the field of international development—to help make the world more just, sustainable, and fair. At any given moment of my adult life, you could find me in some version of one of those responses. From being in overly-zealous activist mode, grinding myself down and driving others away—to drawing the curtains of my bedroom windows shut, covering my ears, curling up in the fetal position, and pretending nothing is wrong.

Maybe you've been there too. Maybe you've felt the exhaustion of trying to stay engaged, or the guilt of wanting to check out. Maybe you've watched community spaces implode, or work projects stall. Maybe you've felt inspired by what's possible one day and totally defeated the next.

If you can relate to any of these experiences, this book is here to say, "*I see you.*" It's my humble hope that this can be a place of reprieve for your experiences with what's happening in the world. That it can help you make sense of the rise in global pain, and talk shop on what to do about it. I hope it's like taking a big sip of Gatorade or coconut water and hearing, "*You make sense… this all makes sense… you're not alone….*" as it goes down.

Because what you're feeling does make sense. We have a new, more intimate relationship with the world. It's a world that's changing fast and in a lot of pain. We see more of who she is—the good, the bad, and the ugly—and know how all of her moving parts interconnect. Never before have we had such a clear, continuous view of ourselves as a global system. And frankly, many of us don't know what to do with this new kind of relationship.

When we don't know what to do with pain and complexity, it's easy to conclude that things have gone terribly wrong. That we're witnessing the end times. That humanity has failed and we're beyond repair. Which, if that's what you're thinking right now, is a fair conclusion.

But what if it means something different?

Here's what I want to offer: what if the world isn't as broken as we think it is? What if all this pain we're seeing isn't so much a sign of our inherent demise, but is actually a sign of our strength? The rise in global pain is our system communicating to us what needs to change—and it is just doing so really loudly. Therefore, it becomes our job to learn how to listen.

Or what about this one: what if the fact that so many collective wounds are in our faces these days actually means that we're collectively resourced enough to heal them? That enough of us have the conditions we need to do so—enough safety, support, and bandwidth. There are the long-held, historical ones related to oppression, and the newfound future ones related to the livability of the earth. The fact that we feel them so deeply gives us an opportunity to heal them. Now we just need the tools to do so.

I'll give you one more: what if the world is in so much pain because we're becoming more consciously aware of ourselves as a system? We can see and sense ourselves more fully as a world. We're waking up to what's possible as a collective, which means that we're also waking up to all the shadows and patterns that no longer serve us, just like in a personal awakening process. Now we just need to clean them up.

These are some healing-centered ways to make sense of what's happening that I like to play with, and that I will invite you to explore with me here. They don't deny the reality of the pain, or pretend that it's not important, but instead offer a shift of perspective. We'll see what we can take from what we know about individual healing and apply it to the collective—as if she was a person—to see what new insights might emerge.

While this perspective shift has spiritual undertones to it, social science research suggests that rising collective anxiety and emotional unrest signal that deeper changes in social order are underway. That these aren't just symptoms of inevitable doom—they're signs that our shared system and ways of being are breaking down to make room for something new. They're part of a larger cycle of renewal. In this view, our emotional responses aren't separate from change—they're part of how change unfolds. They're evidence that our collective consciousness is shifting.

An invitation to approach things differently

Collective healing—as I've come to understand and practice it, and therefore the way I share it with you here—helps us make sense of the rise in global pain and offers us a set of tools we can use to work with what we're feeling. These are healing-centered tools that help us work with emotions in our minds and bodies, seeing them as our inner guidance system, which has evolved over millions of years to help us adapt to change and navigate life.

We work with them because it helps us feel better and stay sane, which is no small feat. Equally importantly, we do so because it will help us show up and respond to all of this change in a more grounded and whole-hearted way. We can better respond with integrity, rooted in our values, instead of being pushed and pulled by the latest whim. We can learn to help our communities, relationships, and society in a way that doesn't abandon ourselves in the process. It will help us to be the people we want to be in challenging times, supporting the shifts happening within our collective consciousness, because we are conduits of the larger system to which we belong.

Collective healing helps us to do this by allowing us to work with the grief, confusion, fear, guilt, or rage that comes with caring about the world. It gives us space to pause and feel—to be human. It helps us notice our protective responses—like checking out or getting reactive—without shame and engage them with curiosity and care.

This is the work that so often gets skipped. Not because we don't need it—but because we're not taught to value it. In our fast-paced, production-oriented culture, slowing down to feel can seem like a distraction from "the real work." But what if it's the opposite? What if this *is* the real work? What if learning how to be with what we feel is what makes genuine social change possible?

These are the questions I've been holding and the work I've been doing through We Heal For All since 2018: offering frameworks and community spaces—such as my We Heal For All Circle model, which you'll see referenced throughout this book—that help people have a healthier relationship with our beloved world. I offer them not just as self-care, but as transformation that ripples out into the world.

Here's where you come in

Whether you're an activist, a concerned citizen, a parent worried about the future, or simply someone trying to be a good person, if you're using your life to positively shape the world around you, then you're a changemaker—and you have a key role to play.

Being a changemaker doesn't necessarily require a megaphone or a seat at the policymaking table. It's often much more subtle work that so many of us are already doing. It's how you spend your money, the food you eat, how you treat the cashier at the grocery store, the way you go about building a family, or how you handle conflict at work. In my view, being a change-maker is about shaping the cultural waters around you by embodying the change you want to see in the world. And it's the kind of change-making we need more of these days.

However, there's a missing puzzle piece in how we're taught to approach change. The dominant pattern goes something like this: become aware of the problem, then try to fix it. Get informed, then take action. And while this model has fueled a great deal of meaningful work, it doesn't account for what happens in between. For many of us, awareness opens a floodgate—we see too much, too quickly, and are left overwhelmed without a clear way forward. We care deeply but often don't know how to hold all of that care, let alone translate it into something meaningful.

At the heart of this book is the understanding that what we're experiencing on the ground—our feelings of stress and distress, rage and heartbreak, overwhelm and helplessness—is directly tied to larger shifts going on for us as a collective. Not only that, but I'll go a step further to say that they're here for a reason. They're an integral part of society's transformation. We just need the right tools that support us to work with them, which is where collective healing comes in.

Whether we realize it or not, we're all participating in the evolution of society simply by existing in this moment. Our feelings, then, are more than something to regulate in order to feel better and get back to normal. They're doorways into vast amounts of information tied to this time of change. They are a connection point between you and the collective body you are part of, and that you are constantly co-creating by the way you live your life.

My intention here

This book is rooted in a simple belief: the times we live in—however painful, confusing, or overwhelming—are not an accident. They are part of something larger. Spiritually and evolutionarily, I believe we're exactly where we're meant to be. Not because it's comfortable or fair or easy, but because the raw material of this moment holds something important—something worth working with. The question isn't *how do we fix it?* The question is *how do we engage with it in a way that supports transformation?*

That's the heart of this book. I'm not here to offer a one-size-fits-all answer or spiritual shortcuts. You won't find promises of peace or step-by-step instructions for solving the world's pain. That's not how this works. And frankly, that's not how life works.

What you *will* find is something more alive, more uncertain, and more attuned to the real complexity of being human these days. You'll find a practice—one that you can make your own. You'll find a perspective—a healing-centered way of seeing the world's pain. You'll also find invitations—to slow down, feel what's present, and explore your relationship with this moment.

For a long time, the subtitle of this book was *How to Be in Relationship with the World's Pain.* But that framing started to feel misleading. It implied there was a neat method, a "how to" that might resolve the discomfort. But this book isn't about resolving discomfort. It's about actualizing the potential within it. About discovering what becomes possible when we stay in relationship with the world's pain—when we listen to it, work with it, and allow it to shape us.

When I say "the world" here, I'm not just talking about geopolitics or headlines. I mean the larger living system we're entangled in: the ecosystems, the communities, the grief, the beauty, the momentum of history, and the inertia of institutions. For many of us, especially in healing and relational spaces, the world is not just an "it" but a "her"—not a symbol or metaphor, but a felt presence we're in relationship with.

This relationship isn't metaphorical either—it's quite literal. To be "in relationship" with something recognizes that you're part of an ongoing exchange. There's a living connection between you and the world—a mutual influence, a dynamic back and forth. What happens out there touches you, and how you respond touches it back. You're not a passive observer, you're part of the interaction. You get to choose how you engage with that connection. And that choice—how you show up, how you listen, and how you act—is what shapes the relationship itself.

So, while there are tools and practices inside these pages, the path they lead you down isn't predetermined. What it looks like for you will be different than what it looks like for me—and that's a good thing. We need multidimensionality in our responses. The goal isn't to arrive at a shared outcome, but to share a commitment: to meet what's here with presence, and to participate in the world's transformation from the inside out.

That's the invitation of this book. To think outside the box. To stay emotionally and spiritually engaged. To co-create meaning in a time that can feel void of it. And to ultimately explore what it means to collectively heal in the 21st century—not as a concept, but as a practice that meets this moment in all its complexity.

This is the opportunity that this work inspires in me and that I humbly invite you into through this book.

I'm so grateful you're here.

A note on support

Since topics in this book touch on trauma—personal and collective—I want to encourage you to take care of yourself as you read (*and in your life all around*). You have complete veto power here—meaning you make the call on what you take in and what you take home. Take breaks, skip ahead, come back later, and, most of all, reach out for support if something touches a nerve you need help holding.

For more gentle suggestions on ways approach this book see Appendix A.

OPENING THE CIRCLE

Inhale.

I'm taking a deep breath in.

Exhale.

I'm exhaling it out.

If we were in a workshop together right now, I'd begin by taking a moment to look around the room to notice everyone around me—the different energies, different faces.

I'd name what I was doing, and invite you to do the same—to gently take each other in, in whatever way you feel called to do so.

It'd be the first moment of many where we'd extend our presence towards each other. Connecting in that subtle, unspoken way—simply with our attention.

This light opening ritual—of gently offering our attention towards each other—is always quite grounding for me. It brings me into my body and into the room, noticing the other bodies and beings in the room and what it's like to be with them. It cues me that I'm entering something shared.

While we're not in a physical room together, I'm imagining that's what we're doing now—across space, across time—in our own unique way.

Maybe for you that looks like checking in with your body, or noticing the room or environment around you . Using it as a brief moment to connect with yourself as we move into the book.

I'll do the same on my side, taking a breath as I do.

As we move through this book, you'll notice that I invite you to stay emotionally connected to yourself as you go, just as I did here. There will be pause points—reflection prompts and moments for you to check in with yourself that you're welcome to use as you please.

At the core of this is the invitation to bring the intelligence of your body, heart, and spirit into the mix. To notice what you notice as you read, and hold that as equally interesting and important information to your thoughts and mind. What subtle shifts happen in your body? What memories or images surface? What lines make your heart skip or your chest tighten? These are ways your wisdom speaks.

Below I share a guided meditation to help you set up this connection point between you and your inner world. Come back to it as often as you'd like.

I'm placing my hand on my heart and taking a final deep breath.

And with that, we're officially opening this workshop-of-a-book together.

Guided meditation: *How are you, right now?*

Grab your headphones and scan the QR code below for the guided meditation.

Ask yourself: *What's present with me right now, in this moment as I begin this book? What's my mind like? My emotional landscape? My body?* Try noticing without judgment, simply taking it in with curiosity.

What is your relationship with the world like these days?

Not in an abstract way, but in your lived, everyday life. What does this relationship look and feel like for you? In what ways does it show up—in your relationships, work, or mental health—and affect your life?

If we're thinking about this book as a workshop, what do you want to bring with you into the space that might serve as a guide?

It could be a question, a longing, an itch at the back of your heart, or a sense you feel stirring deep down. No need to name it concretely. The invitation is to lightly hold it as you read, not as a problem to solve, but as a guide that might reveal something to you.

Chapter 2

MY STORY

'd like to start by sharing my story with you.[1] It's my own journey—an ongoing one—of figuring out how to be in relationship with the world's pain, and it's the origin story of the way I've come to understand collective healing.

This isn't just a personal healing story, though that's part of it. It's about my evolving relationship with our changing world—a journey that I believe mirrors things that many of us are experiencing these days. In my case, it's a journey from righteous anger to something better resourced, and closer to being whole—from spitting fire to learning how to sit in the fire.

Over the course of nearly 20 years, I've gone from being a headstrong activist who saw injustice everywhere, to a systems thinker working at the root causes of issues, to a collective healing practitioner helping others—and myself—find ways to stay engaged with our hurting world without burning out or going numb.

What follows is an ongoing journey of transformation—the subtle kind that happens through years of reckoning and recalibration. The kind that unfolds alongside a world that keeps shifting and cracking and asking new things of us.

---

1   For those who want to know more about who I am and where I'm coming from (i.e. my identity and background), I've shared that in Appendix B.

Maybe, as you read, you'll see glimpses of your own story in mine. In whatever ways you it resonates or doesn't, I appreciate you being here and holding it with me.

So grab yourself some tea and a blanket. Let's begin.

Awakening to injustice

I don't know about you, but I'm a "feeler."

I've always been this way—deeply connected to my emotions and inner world. It's just how I'm wired. Some people like me identify as empaths, others as highly sensitive people or clairsentient. "Feeler" has worked for me. It's like I just naturally feel and sense things at a deep level, which means I spend a lot of time exploring my inner world; and I have needed to get clear on where it ends and the rest of the world begins.

It was the feelings that I felt the first time I learned about extreme poverty that set me on a path of pursuing social justice and international sustainable development.

My memory of it is vivid. It was my sophomore year of college. I was 20 years old, sitting cross-legged on the grass on the main campus quad between classes. The fall air was crisp, and the sun was warming my back. I was poring over some mandatory reading for one of my liberal arts requirements—an article about extreme poverty in Sub-Saharan Africa by Columbia University Professor Jeffery Sachs.

It was full of statistics, like the fact that half of the population there lives below the international poverty line of $1.25 a day, and anecdotes about mothers not being able to prevent their young babies from dying from things as benign to my way of life as diarrhea.

The weight of this reality fell over my whole body like a thick, wet blanket. It was my first real encounter with just how deeply unfair and unjust the world is—how many people lack even the most basic necessities. Sitting in my cushy campus environment, the stark contrast hit me hard. It was an awakening moment. My outlook on things changed forever.

You see, up to that point I had had my sights set on pursuing a career in psychology. I shadowed psychiatrists in high school, had a keen interest in neuroscience, and had been low-key diagnosing people around me with different personality disorders for years (*this last line is a half-joke*). I've always had a natural knack for listening and being of service to others in this way. It's actually why I started a coaching practice in my adult years—so I could send the strangers I meet on the subway who end up telling me their life story to my coaching practice.

Reading that article shifted things for me in a big way. As my mind took in all of this new information, a tsunami of emotional energy washed over me. The mother's eyes in the article's images carried such a deep, universally recognizable exhaustion. It's as if they held generations of structural fatigue—the relentless cycle of material poverty showing its marks. The article transported me to another part of the world and another way of life that was so very different from my own. Heavy sadness landed with a thud in my chest. Righteous indignation rose from my belly. Fiery tingling emanated from my arms and face. I was activated.

"Woah!" I thought to myself, as I noticed these intense sensations coursing through my body. *"Now this is interesting."* The nerdy psych major in me continued, *"If I can figure out how to sublimate this energy and channel it in some sort of constructive way then I think I could be on to something!"* Cue my pivot to sociology!

The more I learned about the world, the angrier I became. Everywhere I looked, I'd see the source of my hurt—blatant injustice, discrimination, objectification, oppression. No element of society seemed to be untouched.

On top of that, I felt very alone. Why can't everyone else see what is going on? Why aren't we all revolting? This was 2008—years before "woke culture." I had a few fellow comrades, like my friend Jenn who picked up what I was putting down. We were the ones who would storm out of parties when racist jokes were told, or leave movies early when homophobic slurs were thrown around for cheap laughs. We were seen as "radical," with friends apologizing to others for our off-putting behavior. It was isolating.

I didn't know what to do with my anger and newfound awareness of the world. It was like a ticking time bomb that would detonate at any sign of transgression. There was an air of superiority within it. The only way I could make sense of everyone else's complacency was by writing them off as ignorant. The judgment was its own form of coping with the isolation and overwhelm. It became harder to relate to family members and old friends. The only thing I knew how to do was to channel all of that anger into taking action. I marched in protests, organized campus demonstrations, volunteered at inner city schools, and worked my butt off to learn as much as I could about the ways of the world.

Throughout this whole period, I didn't know what else to do except to give. To give my time, my money (which I didn't have), and my professional career to the cause of disrupting systems of oppression and structural inequality. Those terms just rolled off my tongue because of how much I identified with that mission. My sense of self became so wrapped up in being of service to the world that I began to get lost. All the emotional energy I was carrying as I pursued this path was unbearable at times. How could I hold the weight of the world?

I remember sitting on a bus one day on my way to a conference. As we drove down the highway, I watched the billboards going by, one by one. Each one was demonstrating the reality I knew so well at that point—that systems of oppression were inherently baked into the fabric of our society. A make-up ad with a big-boobed, white, blonde woman telling me what the norms of sexuality are. The ads themselves were capitalism manipulating me into spending money on things I didn't want or need!

As the dagger-filled anger continued to boil within me, a small inner voice stepped forward and encouraged me to soften my eyes. *"You won't last if you don't."* I sighed. I knew what this part of me was encouraging me to do. If I kept up such a harsh gaze on the world, I would burnout, at best, or go crazy. But how could I soften my eyes when all I saw was that hurt? How could I remain present with the reality of our grossly unequal world without being angry?

I didn't have answers to those questions yet, but that little voice would keep showing up for me over the years to come, gently nudging me towards finding my own answers.

Learning the system

A big chapter in my "fiery activist" phase was moving to Nairobi, Kenya to work for a housing and education organization called Harambee Youth Kenya. When it came time to graduate college, I knew I wanted to volunteer abroad for a year, and had a placement lined up in the Philippines through a prominent faith-based organization.

Then something surprising happened. I visited the boys at Harambee Youth Kenya, an organization founded by my friend, who had grown up homeless in that same area as a kid. Arriving on the ground, I saw that the organization was struggling—the boys hadn't eaten for three days, supplies were being siphoned off, and several boys were out of school. My heart broke and my fire went into action. I had to do something. So I ended up dropping my plans for the Philippines and pivoted to help in any way I could.

I worked stateside, helping to set up a nonprofit organization and fundraise, while simultaneously working three nanny jobs to save enough money to move my boyfriend and I to the Dagoretti Market, where the center was. We lived down the street from the boys in a one-room house with the program manager. Wide-eyed and bushy-tailed, I threw myself into the work of putting my vision of justice into action.

However, my time there quickly showed me that I needed more than a bleeding heart to get stuff done. We tried to get an aquaponics project off the ground, but failed. I was able to bring stakeholders together—from the Ministry of Fisheries to local restaurants to other community-based projects in the region. Unfortunately, my ability to pull all of it together—the finances and operations—was sorely lacking.

I needed more hard skills. The passion that had carried me to Nairobi wasn't enough on its own to create real change, and I was beginning to see that. So I decided to go back to school. I pursued a master's degree in international development practice, a program that brought me full circle back to that original Jeffery Sachs article that had set me on this path years earlier. I even ended up working directly with Professor Sachs after grad school, at a UN think tank called the Sustainable Development Solutions Network.

Through this program and the professional years that followed, I dove headfirst into the "belly of the beast," as I endearingly say, to learn the institutional landscape of the international community and how to create impact at scale.

Those years were great for me in so many ways. I was surrounded by super smart, badass people from all over the world who were called to work at the societal level, just like me. I was exposed to everything from early childhood development initiatives in rural India to anti-corruption programs in Kazakhstan to food security innovations in Argentina.

One of the most valuable things I gained was learning how to think in terms of complex systems. I learned to approach issues like food insecurity or youth unemployment from a whole-systems lens. This meant understanding not just the symptoms, but also the root causes and larger systemic context that any issue exists within, then carefully testing which acupuncture points might create meaningful change.

This systems perspective enriched my approach to social problems. It showed me how cyclical and interconnected global issues and systems are. What are the downstream effects of this policy decision? What happens three steps after we intervene? What historical or geopolitical forces are keeping this problem in place?

Not only that, but those years also brought all of the ideas I had learned in college down to earth. I was getting real world experience and it was humbling. Far from confirming my ideas, field work challenged them at every turn. I got into the nitty gritty of large-scale projects and saw how hard—truly hard—it was to get things done. The slow pace of bureaucracy, the messy reality of working in teams, the constant operational hurdles, funding constraints, endless red tape and more.

It brought me face-to-face with the entrenched nature of so many of these problems, and the inevitable trade-offs and unintentional effects that any solution brings. What looks straightforward on paper becomes exponentially more complex in practice.

I walked away as a specialized generalist in the field of international sustainable development—someone who can diagnose societal problems and design evidence-based solutions to them. More importantly, though, I walked away humbled. My sense of the world expanded, and my calling to be of service became more grounded and realistic.

Those years revealed something else, too—they reinforced my understanding that certain types of intelligence are more highly valued in our professional world than others. I was running in circles with aspiring government officials, UN diplomats, and data scientists, where a distinctly masculine approach ruled the day: logic-driven thinking, top-down leadership, and domineering forms of relating to people. There was a culturally predominant way to operate as a changemaker that felt increasingly misaligned with who I was.

However, what struck me most was what was missing. Despite their impressive credentials and badass veneers, I could see how working on exponentially large and existentially challenging topics took a toll on my colleagues. I remember one of them sitting in my office at the UN think tank I worked at after grad school. His head was in his hands as he recounted the dizzying reality of the Syrian war, desperately overwhelmed. Another colleague couldn't get out of bed for a full day after the murder of Philando Castile. These weren't isolated incidents—they were glimpses of a larger pattern.

I began noticing a significant gap in our field. For all our sophisticated tools to understand complex systems, and for all the talk about taking a whole-systems approach to economic development, we weren't taking a whole-systems approach to the development of us as practitioners. We didn't have tools or frameworks that addressed the inner dimension of doing this work, which included processing grief and grappling with moral quandaries. We were expected to analyze, plan, and implement—but never to feel. Seed-like ideas for how to fill this gap began to sprout, which eventually became the foundation for We Heal For All.

When personal meets political

My journey from fiery activist to systems thinker took place over ten years. This decade of my life was also marked by a different kind of awakening—a personal one. It was the beginning of consciously healing my own wounds, and eventually understanding how they relate to collective ones.

From an early age, I'd been sensitive to the disruptions in my household. Like all families, mine held beauty and strength alongside pain and trauma.

I knew this even as a teenager, but it wasn't until college—when I was in a new place, away from my usual patterns—that the full weight of it started to make itself known in my system.

Sometimes it would hit without warning: I'd find myself on the floor of my room, face down in what felt like an unrelenting pool of darkness. These depressive episodes would come out of left field and swallow me whole. For a few weeks, I would feel solid, even strong. Then, like clockwork, I'd be pulled back into the underworld of my own psyche.

I didn't have tools to navigate it. I'd self-medicate with weed, TV, partying—anything to get through. I didn't have a strong connection with myself, because to do so hurt too badly. Wounded parts I had been carrying my whole life, including some that rippled back generations in my family line, were making themselves known. It was a jumble of threads. My system was completely overwhelmed.

As a sensitive soul and feeler, it was as if life was looking me square in the eyes and saying, "Learn how to dance or be eaten." So I laced up my shoes and started to learn how to dance with the wounds I was feeling, taking conscious steps towards my own healing.

I started working with a spiritual advisor and began exploring practices like yoga and meditation. Being at a Jesuit university, I was introduced— often reluctantly—to practices of spiritual reflection and discernment, which invited me to explore what spirituality meant to me personally. The first time I recognized Spirit I was in East Africa. I was 20 and on a cultural immersion trip to Tanzania. It was there, on that beautiful soil, that I saw how my Guardian Angels and Spirit Guides had been protecting me throughout my whole life. That even in times of loneliness and fear, they were there. Being shown this in Tanzania left an indelible mark on me and a lasting love for that country.

No part of my healing process was straightforward or easy, and it certainly wasn't linear. The next five years of my life were filled with revelations and backsliding. The cloak that had kept me disconnected from myself slowly began to lift. And when I say slowly, I mean *slowly*. It was more like the corners of the curtains had been grabbed, and like that parachute game I played in gym class as a kid, the curtain would lift—granting momentary awareness and possibility—and then be forcefully brought back down, bringing with it a burst of air that rippled across the fabric. Each time this happened, a new little window formed at the bottom edge of the curtain that I could now peek past.

Years into this slow unveiling, with the curtain still heavy but loosening, I arrived at Zen Mountain Monastery for what I thought would be just another retreat. It was a week-long silent meditation at the Buddhist Temple I occasionally practiced at in upstate New York. I find silent meditation retreats to be deeply purifying and freeing—once I move through the resistance and challenges that undoubtedly arise.

This time around, though, I was having a harder time going through the resistance than usual. It was hard for me to be still. I kept getting waves of nostalgia: cravings for cozy childhood foods, like grilled cheese; or the feeling of being wrapped in a warm, soft blanket instead of upright and exposed in a cool, open temple. I didn't know what was up but, when in doubt, I just kept returning to my practice.

I was sitting in line to speak with one of the Zen teachers during a short opportunity within the retreat to ask questions or receive guidance. There, with fewer people around, I really couldn't let my inner agitation show. I straightened my spine, turned my gaze inward, and just practiced. I was determined not to disrupt others.

That's when a sudden image of myself as a little girl came forward. I recognized her well. She couldn't have been more than six years old, with her little bob haircut and a missing tooth in the front of her mouth. All of the dots in my body began to connect. The feelings that had been coming up over the last several days—the nostalgic longings, my inability to sit still. This image began answering questions I had been holding for years. It confirmed a felt sense suspicion that lingered in my mind and had been at the heart of my healing journey. Here was the personal evidence I needed.

I could no longer contain what I was feeling. I burst out into tears and began sobbing right there on my cushion. The sound of my pain rang through the carefully laid silence. I removed myself, and the head Zen teacher and I sat together for awhile. She was gracious and understood without needing details. I ended up going home early to give my younger self that grilled cheese sandwich and warm blanket she needed.

A week later, I was beginning to feel less raw and more together. I was back at work and the world continued to keep moving, including with a national election that looked like it'd be an easy win for my candidate of choice. Yes, this was the Clinton vs. Trump election of 2016.

Going into election night, my metaphorical champagne bottle was already partially popped. We were about to elect the first female president, and the parts of my body that were so viscerally connected to the structural struggles it had taken to get there were ready to be redeemed and to celebrate.

Then the numbers started rolling in. State after state turned red. The reality that I needed to shelve that champagne bottle and turn to some hard liquor became imminent. I was at an election watching party with many people I didn't know. Once the results became clear, I ran out to my car and bawled.

The raw space in my heart I had felt a week earlier was ripped right back open and stretched further this time. Any semblance of feeling "more together" was out the window as the reality of who had just been elected president set in. The pain related to my personal wounds and the wounds of the disenfranchised world became so loud within me.

In the days and weeks that followed, my anger and hurt consumed me. It was as if I was tapped into multiple pain bodies at the same time, all of them coupling and overlaying with each other. There was the pain in my own body related to my personal history that had recently become clearer. There was the pain in my country's body related to our shared history and the chasm that had just grown. There was the pain in the global body due to a shared history of inequality.

Then there was the pain in my family system and its collective body, as the political divisions in our country manifested themselves there too. Stark red-blue lines were drawn and the narrow-minded daggers of judgment flew across them seamlessly. On the surface it was all about politics, but one only had to scratch what was there lightly to see that it was all serving as an outlet for deeper, unresolved family pain.

I didn't have language for it at the time, but I was experiencing a collapse of boundaries between personal and collective wounds. I couldn't tell where one ended and the next began. Was I devastated because of what this meant for my country? Absolutely. Was I also reeling because it echoed patterns of injustice and powerlessness from my own life? Yes. To me, Trump represented everything I had been fighting against for years—the casual violence against women, the marginalization of "others," and the glorification of domination and control. The experience of it all was a cacophony of noise, pain and confusion I didn't understand.

I found myself at a loss about what to do. I was so passionate and clear about my stances. I needed to take action, both to channel what I was feeling and to make sure it would never happen again. The problem was that the only tool I knew how to use to do this—my ability to communicate—wasn't available to me. Any conversation with a politically divergent family member crashed and burned quickly. They just consisted of emotion-filled one-liners and accusations. No one had the ability to settle their own nervous systems, listen, and converse. Exchanges were heated and filled with a low simmering hate.

My back was against the wall. If I couldn't have healthy, safe conversations about this stuff then it was clear that I was shit out of luck. The fiery passion of my college years when I would snap back at bros in class who would say dumb misogynistic stuff was still strongly with me, and was the main set of tools I was deploying. I had been in my liberal, NYC bubble for so long I hadn't needed to develop any new ones. But I saw how incomplete this approach was and how it didn't jive with the other things I was learning in my pursuit of personal and relational healing.

That's when I knew what to do. I needed to get my ass back into therapy.

Instead of taking to the streets (although I was there for that big Women's March) or diving into organizing mode, I turned inward. I realized I couldn't fight the system anymore. Not the way I had done in the past. I had to take a different approach, and that approach began with me.

Launching We Heal For All

By this point in my story, a new question had arisen—one I felt palpably but didn't know how to articulate: *How do we stay in relationship with a world that's in pain?* I hadn't heard people talk about the emotional toll of being awake to the world's suffering. But I was seeing the need for this conversation everywhere—in my work, in my relationships, in my own experience—with few tools or frameworks to help make sense of it.

Professionally, I could see the cracks in the system. I was surrounded by brilliant, committed people who genuinely wanted to make a difference— but no one had the tools to face the emotional toll of the work. We were all steeped in stories of harm and injustice, yet most of the field insisted on staying at the surface-level—focused on policies, funding models, and strategic frameworks. Anything intangible, anything emotional or spiritual, was sidelined. We couldn't measure it, so it didn't matter.

Except it *did* matter.

I saw colleagues burnout, go numb, or get stuck in cynicism. Behind the spreadsheets and PowerPoints were human beings carrying a lot, without the space to process any of it. In the absence of that space, we were unintentionally reproducing the very power dynamics we were trying to change—top-down control, domination masked as strategy, and technocratic detachment in the face of suffering. Not all the time, but enough that it stood out.

Meanwhile, something inside me was also shifting. I had been on a conscious healing journey for years, learning how to dance with the material I had inherited and the puzzle pieces that made me up. What came up during the meditation retreat had pierced something open. And the side-by-side timing of the 2016 election didn't feel like a coincidence. It was as if my life path was positioning me to see the interrelatedness of these different pains. I could see the fractal-like way that my own personal pain echoed the collective pain, and how the collective pain rippled back down, widening the personal.

All of these things—the flashback at the retreat, the dynamics in my family, the confusion and unrelenting pain in my communities—were showing me that my anger and hurt about the abuse and injustice in the world were directly connected to my own personal experiences of injustice in my life. I knew that I had such a visceral connection to the terrible things I saw outside of me because of the wounds that lived inside me, and that I wouldn't be able to move forward in my calling to be of service until I understood those wounds better.

I needed to learn how to untangle the cacophony of pain bodies I was in touch with—to understand where one ended and another began. I could only begin caring for each of those threads appropriately once I started to do that. The intergenerational pain required deeply held space; my community's pain called for expansive care. To recognize which threads of pain were directly tied to my own history and my own body—and which ones were part of society's collective history and the collective body.

I also stopped being able to ignore a spiritual knock at my door. A divine relentless nudge that had always been at the heart of my work—it's what had pushed me to drop my post-college plans, throw caution to the wind, and go to Nairobi. It had been the source of going into grad school, of believing that I could hang with the academics and go into the belly of the beast to be of service.

Now it was pushing me somewhere else, somewhere new. It was somewhere that I didn't have words for yet, but that I had a spiritual sense of. It was risky though, to take this leap, so I dragged my feet on it, until I had lunch one day with my dear friend Dawit.

"You're grey," Dawit said in between bites, looking out over his sandwich. I sighed. He was right, I knew what he meant. I was doing such badass work on paper—working on sustainable development programs, plugged into the UN world, traveling to different countries. But I was also eating takeout every night, numbing out with media, and surrounded by an environment that often didn't reflect my values. I was at a crossroad—exhausted and disillusioned, and quietly grieving work that no longer felt aligned.

So I did it. I took the leap and left my 9-5 job. I got my savings and a loose game plan in place—freelance work while I made the pivot. In 2017, I jumped. I didn't have a business model or defined method yet; all I had were questions: "What is collective healing? And what does it offer these changing times we live in?"

I knew, deep in my bones, that healing was more than just personal. It had a role to play in the collective realm. I felt called to explore what that meant—not as a concept, but as an embodied practice. And so I began.

In 2018, I founded *We Heal For All* as a container to explore all of this in. It started with experiments in the climate change space, where conversations about psychology were growing. I began developing the We Heal For All Circle model as a tool for processing emotions related to the world. Inspired by Indigenous and women's circles, as well as the cool cutting-edge research about emotions and interpersonal neurobiology, the Circle model uses meditation, storytelling, and resonance practice to help people connect with themselves, each other, and the world at large. In Circle (which is the way I like to talk about it—implying "Circle" as its own thing), we slow down, come into our bodies, and share from the heart about what we're grappling with in order to unearth wisdom and collectively heal.

Once I opened my doors to this work, the need for it revealed itself to me again and again. When a colleague from grad school approached me about bringing the Circle model to her Brazilian nonprofit organization Youth Climate Leaders (YCL), I saw just how necessary these spaces were. YCL's mission is to empower and equip young Brazilian people to be climate leaders. They bring participants in, teach them the science and statistics about climate change, and introduce them to job opportunities. What they didn't account for, though, was the emotional impact that the newfound understanding would have on participants. One young woman couldn't stop crying during the first session. This wasn't just information overload— it was a reckoning with our shared future, and there was nowhere for that pain to go until we integrated the Circle model into their program and created space for it.

The transformation I witnessed through the Circles was humbling and so cool to see. One workshop with the Sunrise Movement—a youth climate advocacy group—comes to mind. At the end of the workshop, in which I gave a presentation on climate anxiety and used the Circle model to help participants work with it, a young man came up to me to share his experience. His eyes were warm and bright, which told me his heart was open. He said, "That experience… it's like when you're a kid and you get lost in the grocery store, and when you go to find help, you realize that everyone's on your team." It was so beautiful to hear. His feeling of isolation had shifted into connection.

Looking back, I can see how so many things converged in founding We Heal For All: the gap I witnessed in my professional field, the intimate work of untangling personal and collective wounds, and the spiritual calling that had been guiding me all along. I had found my way of being of service by helping people stay in relationship with the world without being overrun by her pain. I began supporting people's inner worlds, not just for their sanity, but also for the well-being of the world.

Collective pain explodes

Stepping into We Heal For All and my spiritual calling felt blissful, even euphoric at first. It's that "ah-ahhhh" feeling, as if all the things around me were lighting up and cheering me on. But in classic spiritual fashion, this didn't last long. Spirit turned to me and said, *"Alright, my girl. You ready? Strap up. Let's get to work."*

Cue the 2020s.

A few years into exploring what collective healing looks like in practice, the world cracked open. The pandemic. Lockdowns. Uprisings around racial injustice. January 6th. Information ecosystems splintering. Isolation deepening. A political landscape melting sideways. It felt like everything was unraveling all at once—and I found myself trying to be of service to a collective that was riddled with pain.

In some ways, it validated my work. People who had once looked at me with confusion now said, *"Oh… I get it."* But the work itself became harder, messier, and more complicated. I was offering regularly scheduled Circles on climate change, the pandemic, and racism—but found myself being asked to practice what I believed in a context I didn't feel prepared for.

The effects of all this pain were everywhere. People were doing their best to find their footing in a world that was suddenly upside down. Across the political and social spectrum, emotions ran high—fear, grief, urgency, outrage, and a deep need for clarity. Some doubled down on personal freedom, others on collective safety. Some reached for moral clarity, others for defiance. Some tuned it all out in order to self-preserve. Everyone was trying to figure out how to respond, and in the process, division widened. What began as difference hardened into division. Social trust eroded. And the space between us started to break.

I watched people all around me dig in more deeply to their beliefs—not just as ideas, but as lifelines. Whether it was refusing to wear a mask as a stance against government overreach, or aggressively trolling others who didn't put a black square on their profile picture in solidarity. We were all on edge, doing whatever we could to try to find solid ground, often by drawing hard lines in the sand.

In the progressive spaces I was part of, people were especially on edge. We were fresh off of four years of Trump, in the beginning of the pandemic, and at the height of the Black Lives Matter protests. We were trying to metabolize collective trauma in real time. Newcomers to political awareness scrambled to prove they were learning fast enough, while people who had been in the field for years were overwhelmed and exhausted. A deep moral imperative emerged: to be good, to be on the right side of history, to do and say the right things—and to distance oneself from anyone who didn't. Friend groups imploded overnight. People got dogpiled online for slightly contrarian takes. I saw people lose jobs over social media posts, be removed from parent groups for "wrong opinions", or constantly edit themselves out of fear. The emotional pressure was immense—and in that climate, the difference between disagreement and harm began to blur.

Then I experienced firsthand what I'd been witnessing around me. The very dynamics I'd been observing from the sidelines—the callouts and ruptures that turned political disagreements into personal consequences—suddenly had me in their crosshairs.

It started with a piece of writing I'd shared—something trying to be nuanced about the collective trauma stuff I was seeing. An old friend objected to my perspective, believing it was harmful. I listened, reflected, and landed on us needing to agree to disagree. We had different philosophies, and in my mind, that's okay.

What began as a disagreement took a sharp turn, though. She launched what felt like a personal campaign to discredit me—sending PSA-style messages to mutual friends, contacting my workplace, and even leaving negative reviews on my business page as if she was a client. Even though it was one person, the public nature of it within the heightened climate was deeply destabilizing.

I was pushed and pulled by a thousand inner threads: deep pain around social injustice and the feeling of complicity, just by existing in the world.

My need to belong and be understood. My desire to be good and liked. My sense of self as a progressive, a champion against the very harm she was accusing me of. And disillusionment with a movement that had once felt like home.

Something else was there too, though. A steadier set of threads I'd been cultivating through my healing work. The ones that could recognize when dynamics felt off, or when genuine care was getting tangled up with unhealthy attachment. The ones that were learning to set boundaries and honor sovereignty. And the ones that were rooted in a deeper set of questions about what it truly means to be inclusive—including everyone's right to speak, feel safe, and be different.

The experience became a crash course in collective healing, pushing me to get crystal clear on my values around something murky, complicated, and painful. I could feel the old and the new versions of me colliding, pushing me to shed—deeply shed—certain things I'd been holding that no longer held up: like a zero-sum mentality about privilege, or ways my fear of conflict was at odds with my need to be truthful. I also needed to get clear on the things that I wanted to root myself in more firmly: healthy dynamics in political discourse, movement spaces that didn't replicate patterns of division in their fight for equity.

That period, painful as it was, became a turning point. The spiritual and psychological growth I had been doing was asking me to change. It was stepping forward not just to protect me, but to guide me toward something more aligned with who I was becoming.

I found myself applying the very tools I'd been developing on myself: creating space (a lot of space) for all I was holding—through therapy, select friends, family, and my partner. Untangling different layers of my experience—personal, interpersonal, social—to better understand all that was there. Grappling with parts of me that were seriously at odds with each other. Identifying old beliefs that were no longer of service. Learning my hard nos and where there was flexibility. Ultimately allowing myself to stretch, grow, and be molded by the moment.

While the personal side hit hard, what fascinated me more was the collective pattern I saw playing out. In a strange way, it felt like I was facing a younger version of myself—that fiery activist in college who would storm out of parties—but now scaled up to a cultural level. The same righteousness, urgency, and inability to hold nuance that I had once embodied was now embedded in the culture all around me, and currently being weaponized in my direction. It was a hall-of-mirrors moment for me. The 2016 election had already shown me that my old approach to social change had limits. But this experience showed me what it felt like to be on the receiving end of it—and it was pivotal.

The beauty of it—especially from a collective healing perspective—is that everything I was being forced to process wasn't just for my own sake. It was to feed back into my work in the world. I needed to get clear on the type of culture I wanted to create through the We Heal For All workshops and Circles I was facilitating. To identify which schools of thought I wanted to be part of, and which I didn't. To recognize that there are different approaches out there, and I get to choose.

I had big, thorny questions to answer: what kind of culture do I want to create through my Circles and work? What is this Circle space, *really*? A specific Circle comes to mind during the height of the George Floyd pain. It was a Climate Circle, but all was welcomed, and Floyd's murder had just happened. One member spoke of the tragedy and their desire for us all just to see each other as equals. "I just wish we could stop focusing so much on race and just see each other as human beings." I internally tensed. My progressive brain spun: code red! Colorblindness! Harm! I jumped in to intervene, and very clumsily did so, trying to steer the conversation in the way my progressive mind thought was responsible. His demeanor flattened. I was confused. I left that Circle feeling unsure: had that been that the right thing to do?

I had some deep soul searching to do for this work. Was the Circle space I offered a place to push a particular ideology or teach people how to use certain shared language? Or was it something else—something I hadn't quite figured out how to name yet? Could it be something that sees difference not as danger, but as part of the collective field we are learning to navigate? If so, how do we... do *that*?

While these questions were swirling within me, another realization started to form: that collective wounds—like the ones we were all feeling, the ones I first began to see in the 2016 election—are running the show when it comes to politics. I began to see a pattern, whether I was looking at the progressive friend who went after me or my conservative neighbor who sent me YouTube videos about chemtrails and government weather control and got pissed when I "didn't get it." Underneath these impassioned, sometimes belligerent and hurtful reactions were collective wounds—tender, unresolved pain bodies we all tap into to varying degrees. These wounds drive the political and spill over into the relational when left unaddressed.

A new understanding

The political shake-up I experienced in that period—the questions it raised about what values and culture I wanted to create, and my realization about collective wounds—changed how I showed up. I began developing collective healing tools in response to the cultural dynamics I was seeing. Tools that offered an alternative: ways to meet each other in the messiness through somatic and relational practices; tools that don't bypass anyone's pain or trauma, but instead work from a deeper understanding of how to hold it all.

With collective wounds, I began experimenting with how to listen below the surface of people's political positions to attune to a deeper dimension. Instead of getting caught up in arguments about specific issues or trying to convince someone that the way they see things is wrong, I tried to meet them in the collective wounds I sensed they were feeling. I asked myself, "What is the emotional current underneath what this person is saying? How does that reflect what they value and care about? What are they trying to protect?" This became my entry point to connect. When I did this, I began to find much more commonality than difference.

I began seeing that the driver of polarization isn't just ideology—it's unprocessed collective wounds, and it is something deeply human, not partisan. In a time, which as I write this is still happening, when the division in my country feels so stuck, with so little room for change, this realization gave me hope and showed itself as a thread I needed to follow.

These realizations weren't just conceptual. They were personal. They meant showing up differently with family, friends, and strangers—staying in relationships even when the worldview across from me felt counter to my own, or worse, vulgar or heinous. Holding the tension. Letting go of the need to be right. Making room for something else to emerge. Still staying strong in my boundaries—if something did cross a line—but being more willing to soften towards connection as opposed to writing off in the name of righteousness.

I have found myself more politically homeless, as well—no longer neatly falling into one political camp, which feels like a reflection of the times. Yes, I'm still fundamentally progressive and certainly left-of-center—but I'm more solutions-oriented than ideological (*thanks, systems thinker days!*).

There's so much that's being hospiced right now for us as a society—so much that no longer serves us collectively, therefore is falling away. And within that process, I know that parts of what's dying live in me too. That I have inherited cultural patterns that are I am tasked with unlearning and changing. To be honest about that—to allow it to actually happen—requires me to see myself and these times in a particular way. I've learned to position myself internally to stay humble and curious. To see discomfort and scary edges as critically important. To become someone who can let things go as readily as I pick them up.

This is what collective healing has helped me do: hold complexity without collapsing, especially the emotional and moral kind. It has helped me to see the bigger picture, and operate from that perspective, while still staying rooted in the earth beneath my feet, and the unique role I'm meant to play.

It has helped me deepen how I want to live my values, especially inclusion. This value has always driven my social justice work, but my journey has required me to reckon with contradictions—the ways I've dehumanized others in the name of fighting for inclusion. Now, when I'm face-to-face with worldviews that feel heinous, I can see the collective wounds underneath. This shifts the question from "How do I fight this hateful person?" to "How do I respond to the pain driving their worldview without abandoning my commitment to see them as human?"

This is where collective healing as a practice comes in. It helps me navigate these charged moments by creating space for all parts of my experience—including the parts that want to fight. Through solo practice and in

Circles, I've developed a capacity for spaciousness that I can access in the moment—at dinner, or in a passing conversation. Different parts of me can debate each other: the part that wants to pound my fists and say "Stop that! Why are you doing that?" alongside the part that says "Hold steady. Stay composed. Rise above this moment." Each feeling—anger, hurt, hope, possibility—gets room to exist without taking over or being pushed away.

When I create space like this, wisdom emerges from within the tension. Clarity arises about my boundaries, about what this moment calls for, and about larger goals I want to keep in mind. This practice allows me to meet difficult moments in ways that might actually move the needle toward more safety and belonging—addressing the source pain underneath harmful worldviews rather than just perpetuating cycles of judgment.

Ultimately, it has given me tools to show up more fully. It's been as if collective healing herself—as an animate spirit—has been teaching me. And I have had the good fortune to learn and listen.

What emerged

Everything I offer in this book—every idea, tool, and practice—comes from this journey. From my own lived experience. It is also informed by research and study that has clarified and supported it, as well as a lineage of thinkers, healers, organizers, teachers, and guides who have been working on these questions long before me.

Looking back, I can see how that moment on the campus quad—reading about mothers unable to protect their babies—was my first real awakening to a fundamental truth: we are affected by what happens in the world because we're part of it. What happens around us affects us, and in this age of mass global media, that "what" has expanded exponentially. We're no longer just impacted by what happens in our immediate surroundings; we're also impacted by events and energies across the globe.

The type of collective healing that I've come to understand and practice recognizes this impact. We're not separate from the world's pain—we're in relationship with it. And this relationship, challenging as it is, is actually an opportunity.

What emerged from my journey is an understanding of collective healing in two ways. First, it's a practice—a set of tools that helps us work with what we feel. Disentangling pain bodies after the 2016 election, and navigating burnout and disillusionment in my career showed me this so clearly. Our hearts are inextricably tied to the world and our reasons for wanting to be of service to her. Collective healing recognizes this and sees our hearts as a key muscle we can strengthen. It helps us sustain the work and unearth wisdom held within what we feel and the thorny questions we run into—like the ones I came across in the early 2020s—so that clarity and wisdom can emerge that we can bring into our lives.

Secondly, I approach collective healing as a lens—a healing-centered way of looking at the world's pain. Throughout my journey, I began to see the world's pain not just as chaos to solve or systems to fix, but also as a symptom of something larger taking place. Studying spirituality and healing-centered sciences, I began to wonder, "What would it be like to look at the world—and her pain—the same way we look at a person in pain?" What new insights might that offer? How might that help explain certain phenomenon I see, especially at the collective level? This shift in lens—and the insights it offers—has become just as important as the tools themselves. It has changed how I make sense of the world, and that change has shaped how I respond.

As I write this, in the summer of 2025—filled with war, heatwaves, and rising authoritarianism—I share this approach to collective healing with a lot of humility. It brings me into a soft, sober space that even holds doubts. But I think it's in the honesty of that softening—the way it reflects the direness and complex disarray we're in the midst of—that new findings can come through. When everything seems to be hardening and cracking, the spirit of collective healing—as something that strives towards wholeness by including the muck and breakdown—means that something new can come through.

In the chapters ahead, I'll share both the lens and the practice with you. My humble hope is that it helps you see your feelings about our changing world as an essential part of the collective transformation we're all navigating. I hope it helps you process and make sense of the times we live in, so that you can usher in the conscious culture change the world desperately needs right now, and play the unique and vital role that only you can play.

Taking a breath with you here. What was it like to read my story? What did you notice within yourself—your mind, body, spirit—as you did?

Thinking back to what you just read and loosely holding it in your mind's eye, which parts stood out to you? What seems to be staying with you? Is it because it resonated or because it didn't? Maybe it's more of an image or felt sense, than a particular part of the story. Perhaps it's a set of words or phrases. Hold this with a sense of curiosity and see what it might reveal to you about your own story.

PART II:

MAKING SENSE
OF THE WORLD

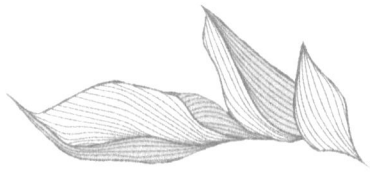

Chapter 3

WHAT WE'RE LIVING THROUGH

We're living through a time of profound change. If you've been feeling overwhelmed, anxious, or disoriented by the state of the world, you're not alone, and it's not a mistake. The emotions so many of us are carrying right now aren't just personal responses—they're part of a larger phenomenon taking place, a transformation not just of systems and structures, but of consciousness itself.

This chapter examines what's happening through a sociological lens. We'll look at data and research that confirms what you might already sense: that we're going through something big as a society—both breakdown and transformation. We'll zoom out to look at the larger forces shaping this change, then zoom back in to explore how they're affecting us on the ground, connecting the dots between the personal and collective along the way.

We'll explore how the "age of awareness" has fundamentally changed our relationship with the world—we see more, know more, and feel more than ever before in human history. We'll examine how this expansion of awareness is disrupting our morals, values, and worldviews, leaving many of us spinning between savior mode and burnout, righteous anger and numbing out. Most importantly, we'll uncover what's missing in how we've been taught to respond to the world's pain—and why that missing piece matters.

By understanding the larger forces at play, and drawing on concepts like collective consciousness and social order, we'll see that our personal struggles aren't happening in isolation—they're symptoms of humanity's larger growing pains. This is foundational for the journey ahead. Because we can't transform our relationship with the world until we understand what's actually happening—both out there and in here.

The weight of the world

"I can't remember a time in my life when the world wasn't falling apart."

Kenlee's words fell out of her mouth in a matter-of-fact way. Leaning back in her chair, the 20-year old went on to describe the enormity and complexity of what she knows about the world. Her hands painted a picture of how big and interconnected it all is; how massive amounts of information feed the mental picture she holds; how there is an inherent pain she feels within it all. It was as if her body was trying to put words to something her mouth couldn't quite form.

She was born after 9/11, into a childhood shaped by school shooter drills, melting ice caps, mass protests, and a near-constant stream of headlines about crisis and collapse. Members of Gen Z like her have grown up with a steady stream of uncertainty which has become part of the emotional wallpaper of her generation.[1]

The timid tone of her voice expressed that she didn't know what to do, let alone how to make any kind of real change. The huge, overly entangled web of it all seemed insurmountable—certainly too complicated for someone to figure out how to fit in within it.

The other 17 university students sitting around the half-moon table with Kenlee resonated with her. They echoed the weight of her words as they chewed on topics like the climate crisis and biodiversity loss, human rights abuses and systemic injustice, the fact that the world population is eight billion and counting, the extreme schisms between the haves and have-nots, the histories that have created these structures in the first place, and the seeming intractability of it all.

Seeing the gravitas the students felt, Chelsea Simpson, professor of the undergraduate class, gently stepped in. *"If you're feeling anxious then it means you're paying attention."*

Like Kenlee, many of us are feeling overwhelmed, helpless, and not sure what to do about the state of the world. A 2023 American Psychological Association survey found that 67% of adults feel overwhelmed by the number of issues America faces.[2] It's the exact kind of thing I see all the time in my We Heal For All Circles. I also see:

People feel utterly alone. *"I've had these feelings my whole life and have never had a place to share them. Like, I have good people around me… great wife, friends. However, I can't talk with them about this. They don't get it. I become an annoying imposition. 'Oh there he goes again…'"*

Others are scared. *"I don't know where to go, what to do, or who to trust. Everything I do is feeding into the things I hate most. I don't even want to breathe out of fear of the butterfly effect."*

Some are angry. *"How the fuck can they do this to us? I can't bring kids into this world! Like, how can I look them in the eyes and tell them I didn't know what was coming as they face so much suffering. War after drought after famine… Like what would I tell them? I'm deprived of having kids because those fuckin idiots couldn't get it together."*

Others are burdened. *"Am I allowed to have a life and do this work? It doesn't feel like it… There's just such an overwhelming sense of responsibility. It's up to me. My generation. We have to fix this! I know I'm doing too much but what else do I do?"*

And then others spin out. *"Such a confusing time in human history. It's exhausting… I find myself just ping-ponging from one thing to another. I'm on edge, in overdrive. There's nowhere to land."*

It's not just you… it's the collective

The stories I hear in Circle reflect just how palpable the world's pain is. It manifests in our work, our choices, our identities… even our sanity. The prevalence of these stories points to something deeper happening—not just personally, but collectively. It's as if the world herself is in pain, and the unrest, disillusionment, and despair are indicators of that.

As psychotherapist and soul activist Francis Weller writes:

"The symptoms are no longer confined to our intrapsychic realities—our personal histories, wounds, and traumas. The patient is now the planet itself, manifesting symptoms of collapse, depression, anxiety, violence, and addiction—felt in the wider body of the Earth, rattling our deep psychic ground, affecting everything."[3]

We are extensions of the systems we are part of—social, economic, political, environmental. Therefore, our personal experiences reflect what's unfolding within the world itself. If we listen closely to the stirrings inside our own psyches, we can begin to sense what's happening inside the collective.

So what are we seeing at the collective level that suggests the world is in pain? Let's examine the United States as one part of the planetary patient.

Feelings about the state of things

How do people feel about where we're going as a world? As of mid-2023, 80% of Americans said they didn't feel good about where the country is headed.[4] Nearly 90% described living through a "constant stream of crises without a break over the last two years."[5]

This isn't just in the U.S. In a global survey, fewer than 10% of people in countries like Sweden and Germany said the world is getting better. The rest? That things are getting worse.[6] These small percentages speak loudly. Widespread unease is one sign of a deeper pain running through the system.

Social unrest

There's nothing restful about our social world right now. Civil unrest—and, in some cases, political violence—is on the rise both in the U.S.[7] and globally.[8] It's one of the clearest signs that the world is hurting: when pain builds up, it eventually erupts.

In a 2022 survey, nearly half of Americans said they wouldn't be surprised if civil war occurred in the near future.[9] That kind of expectation reflects just how unstable things feel. Globally, riots and anti-government protests rose by 244% between 2011 and 2019.[10] Across countries, trust is eroding, and social tension is spilling into the streets.[11]

Political polarization

Polarization in the U.S. is at historic levels—and it mirrors the world's pain. People aren't just disagreeing politically; they're seeing each other as dangerous, immoral, or beyond reason.[12, 13] That level of mistrust reflects a deep rupture.

In one study, over 70% of Republicans and over 60% of Democrats said the opposing party was more immoral than other Americans.[14] Nearly half of Americans say they wouldn't want their child marrying someone from across the divide.[15]

The world's pain drives people crazy. Silos and echo chambers are a natural byproduct of it. When people are carrying unprocessed grief, fear, or rage, it can feel unbearable to stay open to someone who sees the world differently. It's easier to shut down, simplify, or blame. Polarization, in this way, is one way we cope, and the rise of it points to the world being in pain.

Mental health and personal well-being

Indian philosopher J. Krishnamurti puts it best: "*It is no measure of health to be well adjusted to a profoundly sick society.*" As a friend told me, "*I've tried the supplements, changing my diet, exercising... but of course I'm still anxious and depressed. The whales are dying.*"

The world's pain shows up in our mental health. In 2021, 41% of people across 122 countries reported significant stress—the highest ever in Gallup's global polling. In the U.S., deaths from alcohol, drugs, and suicide—what researchers call "deaths of despair"—have doubled in the last decade,[16] and the percentage of Americans in extreme distress has doubled since the mid-1990s.[17] These aren't isolated issues. They're symptoms of a larger stress.

Hope for the future

When people think about the future, worry tends to take the lead. In 2022, 84% of Americans said they were very or extremely concerned about what lies ahead—a trend that cuts across age, background, and political beliefs.[18]

The concerns are widespread. Most Americans expect the country to be more politically divided by 2050.[19] A majority anticipate climate harms worsening in their lifetime,[20] and financial anxiety is on the rise.[21] The overall picture is one of deep uncertainty, which reflects the world's pain.

And yet, glimpses of hope persist. A 2024 UNICEF report found that 80% of adolescent girls worldwide believe their lives will be better in the year ahead.[22] Many Americans, too, report feeling hopeful about their personal future, even while feeling pessimistic about the world's.[23] [24]

That split—between personal hope and collective dread—further highlights the world being in pain. It's as if people feel relatively okay within their personal bubbles, but the moment they expand outward, they encounter something much heavier.

You'd think all that personal hope would add up to collective hope. But it doesn't. And that tells us something interesting.

Taking a breath with you here. What was it like to read through all of this—Kenlee's story at the beginning and these statistics? Depending on who you are and how you are, reading this could have been a lot to take in. Or it could be something you do day-in and day-out. Whatever you noticed, be curious about it, and let it inform your understanding of how you relate to the world and how the world affects you.

What's it like to see the planet as a "patient," as Francis Weller puts it? What's it like to read through these statistics and reflect on them as if the world herself is an animate being?

Shifts in collective consciousness

Feeling anxious after reading that last part? If so, that makes sense. I'm taking a breath with you here. Return to the meditation at the beginning if you'd like, or use it as a springboard to join me in this next section.

Because now I want to talk about collective anxiety.

Social scientists have long noted that rises in collective anxiety—like the ones we just looked at—are tied to shifts in social order happening for a society.[25] A shift in social order means that the way society has been organizing itself no longer makes sense within its current context. It's those planetary boundaries and political edges I mentioned earlier. Therefore the patterns of conduct that we as a society have come to know and love (*well, maybe not "love," but, as a whole, grown accustomed to*) are in the process of breaking down so that something new can arise, which naturally causes widespread anxiety.

This process of breakdown can look like a terminal illness at first glance, but historians assure us that cycles like this are a normal part of how societies operate. Civilizations reliably move through periods of stability—golden eras and cultural flourishing—followed by times of disintegration—conflict, unrest, unraveling.[26] What we're experiencing now isn't unprecedented in that sense; it's part of a larger cycle that can be observed over time.

What's cool is that we even have quantitative data now that maps this rhythm across history. That data confirms what our bodies already know—we're living through one of those times of unraveling.[27] Understanding the larger patterns like this doesn't make the experience any less challenging. If anything, it confirms what we're feeling. But it does offer context. The breakdown of old structures has a purpose—it creates the conditions for renewal. The old order must loosen its grip for something new to emerge. It's how societies evolve.

A society's social order consists of the institutions and structures that hold it together and maintain stability. It reflects the way a society is organized. This includes laws, norms, customs, and social roles that create predictability and help society function smoothly.[28] A social order is reinforced by formal mechanisms, like the judicial system, as well as informal mechanisms, like expectations.

Shifts in social order have traditionally been examined in the context of modernity and post-modernity, and are now being applied to our current era of climate instability and political upheaval.[29] Let's take eco-anxiety, for instance. The fact that a large group of people are experiencing things like climate depression and eco-dread is not only a reflection of changes happening at the individual level, but also—from a zoomed-out, sociological view—a reflection of changes happening at the collective level.

Which brings me to the collective consciousness, a main character in the story I'd like to explore with you.

As a lifelong student of global and cultural systems, the collective consciousness has been a curiosity and teacher of mine since the beginning of my journey. I remember first learning about it in college. I got this image of clouds of energy hovering above different pockets of our world. Some overlapping and interconnecting with each other; others immovable and static. It's like a network of dynamic energy that's undulating in and out of our communities and consciousness. I conjure up a word like "liberty" and see tendrils of energy light up in a cloud that connects to history and the social milieu that my consciousness is personally part of. A term like "healthy living" activates a whole other set of connections to ideas and values and perceptions. The collective consciousness feels sci-fi, technological, spiritual, and sociological all at the same time.

However, I'm getting ahead of myself. The way I'm using the term here is based on the work of French sociologist Émile Durkheim. He coined the term in the 19th century while trying to understand the effects of modernity and the process of cultural change that took place in Western Europe for centuries after the medieval era.

Durkheim defined a society's collective consciousness as the totality of attitudes, ideas, beliefs, and morals that are shared by a group of people and that make up a "social glue" that holds them together.[30] This glue is a body of norms that guides questions like: what's right? What's wrong? What's socially appropriate? What do we consider true? How do we relate to one another? How do we make sense of things?

Part of his work sought to understand how a society maintains its integrity and coherence as a collective when the institutions and cultural practices that make it up vastly change. Sounds familiar, doesn't it?

As a sociologist, Durkheim looked at the collective consciousness as a social phenomenon. He believed that it is something that permeates all aspects of society (family, religion, education, law, healthcare), and that has a life of its own.

As Durkheim puts it:

"There are in each of us, as we have said, two consciences: one of which is common to our group in its entirety, which, consequently, is not ourself, but society living and acting within us; the other, on the contrary, represents that in us which is personal and distinct, that which makes us an individual."[31]

To put it another way, we as individuals embody and enact the norms that are present within the collective consciousness; but when any one of us passes on, for instance, the collective consciousness doesn't die with us. Instead, it lives on as something that's distinctly separate from us as individuals, and is instead an extension of the larger web of society. It exists beyond us.

It's fascinating when you think about it. The idea that the collective consciousness has a mind and life of its own (*my words, not Durkheim's*). That our ideas, beliefs, and morals are not purely our own but are inextricably tied to a collective force that has been in the making since the dawn of time. A collective force that is a product of our decisions as a society, of our history as a people, of the stories we tell, and of the information we have access to.

Social order refers to the structures that govern society's ability to function. Collective consciousness refers to the shared moral-emotional fabric underneath these structures. You could say it's where our sense of self as a society resides. In a day and age when so much is changing so fast, our world's sense of self is in a process of transformation, and we're feeling it. The collective anxiety, fear, and pain are a reflection of her process, and something I humbly believe we can work with to help facilitate this transformation.

Just like how individuals go through identity shifts and experience confusion and discomfort, our collective identity is changing, and the anxiety many of us feel is a symptom of that deeper transformation.

What's it like to see your experiences of anxiety as part of a larger social phenomenon? Does it validate them? Shift them? Perhaps it minimizes them in a way that doesn't feel supportive? Whatever your experience is, it's welcome here, and can be a clue about things you need.

"Collective identity shift." Hearing that term, what does it make you think of? In what ways do you sense, feel, or experience that in your own life? Or in the people and parts of society around you?

The age of awareness

A big driver of these shifts in social order and collective consciousness is the age of awareness that we live in. It's often called the age of information, the age of mass media, or the age of information and communication technology. But I believe that what we're living through is better described as an age of awareness.

Never before have we had such a clear, continuous view of ourselves as a global system—politically, economically, socially, and environmentally. We are waking up to how the world works, to how systems impact people and the planet, and to how deeply interconnected everything is. The good, the bad, and the ugly. That kind of awareness is powerful. And it's also incredibly disorienting.

Information

We are being inundated with more information than any humans before us. The age of information and communication technology—still in its early stages—has given us near-constant access to global news, data, images, voices, and opinions. With the rise of smartphones and social media, we carry the world in our pockets. Events happening thousands of miles away reach us within seconds. Issues that were once invisible or took months to reach us are now vividly present. Moreover, advances in global education, healthcare, and economic stability have expanded our capacity to engage with this information—to read more, think more, and stay connected longer than ever before.

Every point in history is unique in its own way. Our ancestors lived through a myriad of one-of-a-kind circumstances. But what is specifically unique about our time now, is the degree of awareness we have about who we are as a world and what we are experiencing. On the bright side, we are able to learn from peoples, cultures, and traditions in a way we never have before.

Ken Wilber, founder of Integral Theory puts it like this:

"It seems hard to imagine, but for humanity's entire stay on this planet, a person was born into a culture that knew virtually nothing about any other. We live in an extraordinary time: all of the world's cultures past and present, are to some degree available to us, either in historical records, or as living entities in the history of the planet earth."[32]

On the other hand, we are also nose-to-nose with the challenges we face: climate breakdown, mass shootings, bombings and brutal combat, cyber warfare, a growing population, a rise in authoritarianism, species loss, human rights abuses… the list goes on. Heinous, challenging things have always taken place throughout history, but we are the first to have such a front row seat to it all.

I was born in 1988. My formative years were influenced by the Internet: by a surplus of information about every topic one can imagine. It's a tool that can take me to every corner of this world—through images, videos, statistics, and blogs. I am able to live this world like never before. As of 2020, 60% of our global population has access to the Internet. That is 4.5 billion people experiencing the world like in new ways.[33]

This gives us an expanded view of the world relative to any point in history. It means we now have a relationship with information that makes it nearly impossible to turn a blind eye to the world's challenges. To pretend that the choices we make don't matter would be deliberate ignorance. Because the reality is that they do matter and we can find data visualizations that tell us exactly how.

Additionally, the pace and rate at which we are consuming media is at an all time high. It reminds me of the scene from *Matilda* when Bruce Bogtrotter, one of the students at Matilda's school, is forced by Miss Trunchbull, the school's authoritarian headmistress, to eat an enormous chocolate cake in front of the whole school as punishment. He looks sick with indulgence as he reticently scoops handful after handful into his mouth.

This is why when I think about the explosion of information we have at our fingertips today, I can't help but reflect on how it's affecting us as a world; how it's affecting all of those clouds of energy that make up our collective consciousness. Because this is all new for us as a people, especially at this scale, and we're not completely sure what to do with it.

Interconnectivity

Not only are we more aware of various parts of the world, we're also more aware of how those parts are connected. This too is new.

We're developing a systems-level understanding of how things influence and shape one another—the climate and economy, race and housing, conflict and resources, policy and mental health, and so on. This kind of awareness is what scientists and development practitioners call *systems thinking*. It allows us to study the relationships between a system's interacting parts to understand how they produce the collective outcomes we see.

Systems thinking teaches us that the world is more than just the sum of its parts. Instead, it is organized in a way that has a rhythm to it, and if we really want to understand the systems we are part of, we need to understand this rhythm.

The ability to zoom out from a single issue and understand the larger web of factors and forces that create it—as well as how it feeds into other issues—is a key competency of this day and age. We can train ourselves to understand how things like climate change affects crop cycles in sub-Saharan Africa, how policy decisions in the United States lead to political unrest in the Middle East, or how the presence of a mosquito species in Brazil affects global meat prices.

Similarly, it helps us understand that there are no silver-bullet solutions to the problems we face. For instance, we know that reducing poverty is about more than just increasing the amount of money a person lives on each day, although that remains a key indicator of extreme poverty.[34] Truly addressing the cycle of poverty requires tackling issues related to education, healthcare, water and sanitation, roadways and infrastructure, security, and more. Additionally, understanding the context within which poverty exists is equally important. What historical forces and structural dynamics are at play? What is the social and political fabric within which this exists?

Social impact and sustainable development practitioners need to be able to see and engage with the world through this kind of systems lens. But more and more, everyday people are being asked to do so too. Anyone who is plugged into the news cycle, who cares about their local community, or who is learning about different issues and parts of the world is being pulled into this level of complexity.

Developing an awareness of ourselves as a world from this systemic lens is empowering and awe-inspiring, but it is also straight up overwhelming. Creating mental maps and narratives that adequately hold the reality of our interconnected world and highly entangled global issues is a daunting task for the best of us.

Take Sabrina. Some days, she wishes she could turn off her awareness of the system. It's like a dark, simmering cloud that hovers over her head, coloring everything she sees. She goes to her job as a teacher and sees the remnants of segregation in the school districts' lines. She buys her sister a gift on Amazon and shudders at the thought of how it was made.

This type of awareness leaves a lot of us emotionally exhausted and paralyzed—overwhelmed by the never-ending vastness of it all. If everything is connected, what can *I* do that will actually help? If every choice has downstream effects, how can I move about the world without causing harm? If I donate, am I reinforcing the wrong system? If I speak out, am I silencing someone else?

However, within it all, there's also a beauty we can tap into. This system lens reflects what many spiritual traditions teach us about the inherent interconnectedness of all life. We can look out at the vast nature of space and the utterly microscopic nature of atoms and watch them circle back to each other as one. We can feel our inherent interdependence with all parts of the world.

Systems thinking like this is a paradigm shift that comes with a new kind of consciousness. The global nature of our world, its interdependence, and our expanding awareness of how systems behave—all of it is changing how we see reality and how we relate to the world.

Morals, values, and worldviews

We live in a day and age when our awareness of ourselves as a world is at an all time high. Our eyes are open to more, and it's naturally affecting us.

"We are not made for this level of awareness," is something I hear often in my work. People pine for a return to blissful ignorance—some way to un-

know what they now know. And yet, here we are, being asked by the times we live in to figure out how to be in a relationship with all we see.

We can think about this phenomenon in terms of consciousness. Our conscious awareness of ourselves and the world has changed, and with it, our worldviews, morals, and values are being reorganized—both individually and collectively.

"Consciousness" can sometimes be a difficult topic to broach because it can feel elusive and vague. I know I personally can run wild with it, moving from the spiritual to the material to the cosmic… However, for the purpose of our conversation here, let's ground the term as simply as we can:

Consciousness is our awareness of ourselves and the world around us.[35] It's the lens through which we perceive reality, make sense of experiences, and interact with others. At its core, consciousness is about being aware—of our thoughts, emotions, sensations, and the greater context of our lives. It shapes how we:

» Understand the world (our worldviews),
» Make decisions about right and wrong (our morals), and
» Prioritize what matters most (our values).

All of these puzzle pieces interconnect with each other. I think of consciousness as being the larger fabric within which morals, values, and worldviews live. For instance, when someone becomes aware of how factory farming works, that expanded consciousness might make eating meat feel morally wrong. When people first see Earth from space—that pale blue dot—it can fundamentally alter their worldview from seeing separate nations to seeing one unified home. When someone learns about racism's impact on housing or wealth, it can change how they see poverty and shift what they value—from individual responsibility to collective accountability.

Shifts in consciousness aren't abstract. They are happening in real time, in response to what we're collectively seeing and experiencing. Feelings of confusion, anger, and despair are not just emotional reactions—they are symptoms of a deeper, more fundamental disruption to how we understand the world and ourselves within it. They're a natural byproduct of these shifts in consciousness.

If we return to the idea of collective consciousness—the shared set of beliefs, values, and assumptions that shape how a society functions—then what we're seeing now is its active reconfiguration. As that social "sense of self" undergoes transformation, we each feel our own version of that change. We are conduits of the system. Each of us is a node, and our personal experiences reflect the broader shift that's underway. Which also means we can use them as an entry point to help guide change.

Let's unpack morals, values, and worldviews a bit more to see exactly how this plays out.

Morals and values

Our morals and values guide how we live day-to-day. Morals are linked to our ethical compass—what we believe we *ought* to do based on deeper commitments often rooted in religion, spirituality, or philosophy. Values, on the other hand, are more subjective and personally defined. They shape what we prioritize in life—how we spend our time, where we put our energy, and what feels worthwhile.

For many of us, what's happening in society is leaving our morals and values in a disoriented place. We feel confused about what's going on, what's right and wrong, and how to draw clear lines in the sand. Whether it has to do with our government's military spending, handling of illegal immigration, foreign policy—many of us don't land cleanly in one place. Most topics are too complex to do so.

Seeing an issue from multiple sides can cause our values to go head-to-head with one another, leaving us even less sure about what to think or what to do. On one hand, I value inclusion and participatory methods of decision making—having everyone's voice at the table and ensuring they're represented, regardless of background or politics. But, I also value protecting and advocating for groups that have been historically marginalized. Where does that leave me when it comes to permitting white nationalists or right-wing extremists into national decision-making? My values are at odds with one another.

Our morals can be at odds with the way society operates more generally too. This is the terrain of moral injury. It occurs when our belief system no longer matches our experience—when the story we told ourselves about what's right is betrayed by what's real. We go to war to fight for freedom but find that we actually just fought for oil. We value the sanctity of life but accidentally kill someone in a car accident. As Union Theological professor Dr. Rita Brock puts it, "*Our core moral foundations are unable to justify, process or integrate the trauma*"[36] and we're left questioning not just what we've done, but who we are.

Consciousness is what enables moral reasoning in the first place. It allows us to reflect on consequences, feel empathy, and navigate ethical dilemmas. As our consciousness expands, so too does our moral imagination. A more expansive consciousness might widen a person's circle of care—extending moral concern beyond their immediate community to include people across cultures, ecosystems, or even future generations. But this kind of expansion can also come with trade-offs: when we zoom out too far, we can risk overlooking the needs of those closest to us, or feeling immobilized by the sheer scale of what we care about. By contrast, a more constrained or survival-oriented consciousness might focus attention on protecting one's family, community, or identity group. While sometimes dismissed as narrow, this stance can reflect real threats or scarcity, and can serve important functions like resilience, loyalty, or nurturing culture.

Consciousness also shapes the ways we interpret and prioritize our values. Someone with a more individualistic orientation may focus on autonomy, achievement, or self-expression. Someone with a more collective or relational consciousness might emphasize care, equity, or interdependence. Neither stance is inherently better than the other—they just reflect different ways of locating meaning, and each carries wisdom that may be more or less helpful depending on the context. What matters is recognizing that the upheaval we're experiencing is activating these questions for a lot of us—inviting, and in many cases demanding, that we re-examine our morals and values.

Worldviews & existential questions

If our morals and values guide our day-to-day lives, then our worldview is the framework that organizes them into a larger belief system. It's the lens we use to make sense of reality—consciously and unconsciously. It holds our assumptions about existential questions like: what life is, what it means to be human, and how the universe works.

As poet Anaïs Nin wrote: *"We don't see things as they are, we see things as we are."* [37] What we take in is filtered through our worldviews. They run so deep we often don't know we're seeing through them. They are shaped by our upbringing and cultural surroundings, and constantly reinforced by our environment and social context.

Now with so much changing, the assumptions that underpin our worldviews are being shaken up. We find ourselves revisiting basic assumptions we may not have questioned before. What does it mean to be a good person these days? Is it as simple as being nice to your neighbor, or does it require something more? What does it mean to succeed, to own something, or to live well? How do we make sense of suffering, freedom, or truth in a world in flux?

These shifts in worldview are not happening in isolation—they reflect deeper shifts in consciousness. As our awareness expands in response to what we're seeing, our foundational ways of interpreting the world are being stretched. Consciousness and worldview shape one another: as consciousness evolves, so too must the frameworks we use to make sense of reality.

In lockstep with shifts in the collective consciousness, our worldviews are being forced to evolve. When they no longer help us make sense of what we're seeing, they begin to break down—and we are left with the challenging but necessary task of helping them transform. This doesn't mean abandoning all we've known, but it does mean letting go of what no longer serves us, and allowing something new to come through.

All of this—our shifting morals, values, and worldviews—doesn't just affect how we think. It affects how we feel. As we take in more of the world's pain and complexity, we're not just rethinking our place in it—we're trying to hold it all in our bodies and nervous systems. And we each respond in our own way, doing our best to work with what's changing.

Think back to what I said about us being conduits of the system. "Each of us is a node, and our personal experiences reflect the broader shift underway. Which also means we can use them as an entry point to help guide change." What's it like to see yourself this way? What does it inspire or bring up?

How we cope with breakdown

Let's be real. As much as many of us want to show up, have been trying to do so, and are deeply interested in figuring out how to be helpful these days, the majority of us are straight up struggling.

The world is on fire and we don't know what to do. There's no playbook for how to have this new kind of relationship with the world, so we're falling back on whatever coping mechanisms and strategies we can.

Each of us responds in our own way. Some of these responses are loud and fiery. Others are quiet and inward. All of them are creative forms of self-protection in some way. They are ways our mind, body, and heart try to keep us safe and balanced under the weight of a world in change.

Below are some common responses I see in my work and community. They are ways our systems respond to collective pain and uncertainty:

- » Savior mode
- » Burnt out
- » Hot and stuck
- » Untethered
- » Tuned out
- » In a knot

There are no neat lines between these categories, and I wouldn't call the list complete. Instead, they overlap. We may cycle through them over time, or even in a given day. And there are responses—especially nuanced ones—that aren't captured.

Below I share descriptions of each category. This includes depictions of how each response feels—how they tend to show up emotionally and somatically—as well as inner dialogue. They also include the intelligence underneath the response—why it's here and what it's trying to do—the protective wisdom within it.

The invitation is to read through each one and to notice what you notice as you do so. They're written in a way that's meant to speak to your body, not just your mind. So take a moment to check in with yourself here—take a breath, tune into your body—and then gently make your way through them.

Savior mode

You take it all on. This is when you personally shoulder the weight of the world with a Herculean effort. It's fiery, driven, noble—and often unsustainable. Determination and duty overrides all else.

Felt sense
Carrying the weight of the world on your back
Shoulders squared, jaw clenched
Laser-focused
Crushing responsibility
Relentless action
Gotta fix, gotta save, gotta go
Spinning wheels
Determination
High highs and low lows
Overrun, overburdened
Pushing forward, pushing through, breaking down

Inner dialogue
"It's up to me to change things."
"If not me then who?"
"The world's on fire—I can't not help."
"I know I'm doing too much but, like, what else can I do?"

The intelligence within it
I channel my sense of duty and drive to deal with collapse.

Burnt out

You are spent. When you've pushed past your limit for too long, your body shuts down. If you won't take a break, your system will force you to. This isn't laziness—it's exhaustion in its purest form.

Felt sense
> Shoulders slumped, chin tucked in
> Looking down
> Eyes heavy
> Dim, grey
> Collapsed in
> Hands cradling solar plexus
> So tired…
> Energy drained
> Hard to get out of bed
> Body too tired to carry itself
> Shut down
> Disengaged
> Energy folded inward

Inner dialogue
> "I'm just spent, man… to the point that I don't want anyone to talk to me, anything to touch me… I just need to be alone, holed up in my room."
> "There's just a heaviness. I tried and I tried… but I just can't. I have nothing left to give."
> "The compassion fatigue is *reeeaal*."

The intelligence within it
> My body shuts down as a way to tell me that I surpassed my limits. I disengage as a way to protect myself.

Hot and stuck

You're angry. This happens when clarity hardens into righteousness and passion burns without outlet. You fight hard. There's fire here—raw, vital, and strong—but it can isolate you or leave you dry, as it tries to protect what you love.

Felt sense
> Fiercely passionate
> Fire in your belly
> Fists clenched, chest forward
> Righteous indignation
> Shouting from a soap box
> Heels dug in
> Sharp lines drawn
> Bridges burned
> Isolated
> Arms crossed, back turned
> Blinders on
> Full of energy

Inner dialogue
> "Everywhere I look, the crisis is there, staring back at me… grimacing and mocking me."
> "Why aren't we all revolting? Why can't anyone else see this?! No one gets me."
> "Burn it all down!"
> "If you're not with me, you're against me."

The intelligence within it
> My fierce posture and anger protects the depth of my wounds.

Untethered

You dissociate. You are unable to stay present with it all because it's too much. There's a floating sensation—mind spinning, body overwhelmed, nothing to land on. This is what disorientation looks like when the ground falls away.

Felt sense
Exasperated
Unsure
Dizzy and in a daze
Small
Head tilted upwards
Hands in the air
Palms to the sky
Pleading—"what do I do?!"
Looking for something, but seeing nothing
Searching, seeking, failing
Disbelief in self… and in the system..
Floating away
Lost and adrift
Ungrounded, unable to see, unable to make moves
Overwhelmed

Inner dialogue
"I don't know where to go, what to do, or who to trust."
"I care, but who I am to be able to do anything? I can't effect change…"
"I feel like I'm watching everything from outside my body, like none of this is real anymore."
"It just keeps slipping away… As soon as I think I get it, can feel it, have somewhere to land, it just… disappears."

The intelligence within it
When I dissociate, my body and mind create a lot of space within me, so it's bearable.

Tuned out

You opt out. This response distracts, deflects, or numbs. Not because you don't care, but because going deeper doesn't feel safe… or productive.

Felt sense
  Numb, disconnected
  Shut off
  Push it away
  Nahhh… *swipes to the next*
  Turning the music up louder
  No interest, shut down
  Quiet guilt
  Protectively numb
  Detached
  Keeping busy, staying distracted
  Booze, parties, weed, work, sex
  Blunted
  Avoidant
  Untouched, unphased

Inner dialogue
  "None of this really matters, right? The system is totally broken and
  rigged against us anyway, so why even try"?
  "Dude, don't worry about it… the aliens will fix it or we'll just reboot
  the simulation."
  "Nah, let's not go there… Another round!"

The intelligence within it
  Apathy shields me. It keeps me above it all.

In a knot

You are ambivalent. You care deeply, but feel stuck. You're pulled in every direction—between hope and despair, action and avoidance. It's murky and unresolved, but it's alive.

Felt sense
Torn, conflicted
Pressure building inside
A knot in your stomach
Stepping forward, then back… then forward… then back
Frozen
Weary, fatigued
Mind stuck looping
Aching inside
Working so hard to manage
Head in hands in defeat
Possibility and powerlessness, hope and despair… all tangled up
Inner tug-of-war

Inner dialogue
"I care so much it hurts… I wish I didn't."
"I want to do something, but nothing feels right. It keeps me up at night and then I retreat. I don't know what to do"
"I feel resentful and disheartened by all the self-righteousness and performing from people who say they're the only ones who care… and so I overcorrect by turning away. Part of me thinks they might be right, that I don't care enough, so then I feel shame."

The intelligence within it
The inner tug-of-war shows me that I'm emotionally alive but split and stuck. The knot of emotions includes my care.

*Which ones feel familiar to you? What do you recognize in yourself
or the people around you? What responses might you add to this?*

Collective healing: the missing puzzle piece

These (very normal and quite understandable) responses to what we're up
against point to something. There's a missing puzzle piece in our current
equation for social action.

The model we're living in—implicitly or explicitly—goes something like
this: *wake up, then act*. Awareness becomes the fuel for engagement. And
to be fair, this model has moved mountains. People are waking up to the
realities of injustice, extraction, inequality, and collapse at a scale and pace
we've never seen before. They're marching, organizing, donating, voting,
and seeking new ways to live and lead. In many ways, it's working. People
care and want to help.

If you've made it this far in the chapter, though, you already know there's
more to the story. You've felt the weight of what happens after the "waking
up" part—what happens when we see too much, too fast, with no map
for what to do next. As we've explored, the expansion of our awareness is
happening at every level—cognitively, emotionally, morally, and spiritually.
Our sense of self as a collective is changing. Our worldviews on the ground
are shifting. In some respects, our bodies and nervous systems are carrying
more than they ever have before. And in response, many of us are spinning
out. Overwhelmed, paralyzed, shut down, disconnected. Or just trying to
cope the best we can.

These are normal responses to abnormal times. However, they don't always
lead to constructive action. We're seeing a rise in reactivity, burnout, puri-
ty politics, spiritual bypassing, and unprocessed trauma driving public discourse. We're also seeing people give up—detaching from the world, because
staying engaged just feels fruitless or hurts too much. While we may judge
these behaviors in ourselves or others, they make sense when you realize that

what's missing from our current equation isn't awareness or action—it's the space in between. It's the part where we process what we've seen. It's the part where we tend to what's been stirred up inside us while we try to do something with it. It's the part where we metabolize the energy of the world so we can move forward in a way that's coherent, grounded, and true.

This chapter traced the contours of what's happening in our world—from global crises to social breakdown to the deep internal disorientation many of us are carrying. We've looked at the rise in awareness, the shifts in morals and worldviews, the emotional fallout, and the patterns of response that leave us feeling stuck. And now, we've arrived at the hinge point. The part where the question is no longer just "what's happening?" but "what now?"

What now, given all that we're waking up to?

What now, given the pain we're holding?

What now, if we want to stay present in this moment and participate in its unfolding?

This is where collective healing comes in. Not as a replacement for action, but as the ground from which meaningful, sustainable, and relational action can grow. It's what helps us stay human in the face of it all. It's what helps us transform—not just as individuals, but as a culture.

And that's where we're headed next.

Chapter 4

SEEING THROUGH A HEALING LENS

So where do we go from here? Hopefully at this point we're on the same page—or at least you're along for the ride and agree that the world is in pain and many of us are struggling to figure out what to do about it.

Which brings me to a turning point in the book, where we really begin to try collective healing on for size to see what it offers us.

We'll start by doing so at a big-picture level by exploring the question: why is the world in so much pain and what does it mean?

Specifically, we'll do so at the sense-making level. How do we make sense of the rise in global pain? What does it say about the state of the world? And how does applying a healing-centered lens help to shift or shape things?

Grab your cup of tea and sit back. Let's see what a healing-centered lens can offer us about the times we live in.

Are we fucked?

We talked earlier about how the world herself seems to be in pain these days. If I look at our world as being a person who has her own nervous system, it's easy for me to see that there's a lot of fear, anger, sadness, and confusion in it. I see it reflected in our news headlines and political rhetoric, and in the sharp rise in social unrest and political polarization. Collective wounds are up in our faces like they never have been before.

Why do you think that is? Why is our collective nervous system filled with so much emotional energy? Why are we face-to-face with so many collective wounds? What does that say about the state of the world?

When we chew on these questions, many of us understandably arrive at the conclusion that we're, well… fucked. The world is a dumpster fire of a mess and there's no way around it. Trends in fatalistic rhetoric about each year being worse than the last; campaigns that yearn for a better time; a rise in conspiracy theories to make sense of things; dilemmas about whether or not to bring children into the world…

There's an exasperation many of us feel. We throw our hands up in the air in defeat. Why even bother to try? On the other end of that spectrum of responses, we go into hyper-activation mode. Taking it all on. Full speed emergency response. And then many of us oscillate between these two poles on a daily (*errhm… hourly?*) basis.

Yes, so many of us believe that the rise in global pain means the world is inherently doomed. It makes sense to arrive here. Seeing what we see and feeling what we feel… *bad,* so it's logical to think that the world is in a bad place. What else could it mean?

But what if the world isn't as bad as we think it is? What if the presence of so many collective wounds is actually a sign that our system is… dare I say, strong? It's so strong that it can communicate with us really loudly about what needs to change. That's why we can hear her pain so well.

Or what if the world is actually dying? Or if parts of her are, anyway. The parts of her that are ready to transform, that are no longer of service and are therefore in a process of being hospiced and phased out. The world's pain is these parts making themselves known, so we can help shepherd the process. The world's pain isn't a sign of our inherent defectiveness, but is part of a larger, creative lifecycle that all societies go through.

Or how about this one: what if the fact that so many collective wounds are at the surface is because we're actually collectively resourced enough to heal them? Enough of us have what we need—economically, socially, emotionally, and spiritually—for exiled parts of our system to make themselves known. These are the historical ones that past generations weren't able to face. The intergenerational ones that were too much for our families to bear. We are now at a place where enough of us have what we need for these wounds to come out and be seen. No longer hiding in the crevices of society's folds, they offer us an opportunity to heal.

The role of narratives

These are examples of narratives that are born from a healing-centered lens. Ones that take what we know about healing at the individual level—as it relates to emotions, consciousness development, and spirituality—and apply it to the collective. I'll take you through these in more detail soon (*and ask what you think!*), but before I do, let's unpack what narratives are and how they can help us form a vision of what's possible.

The narratives we use to make sense of the world shape how we relate to her and her pain. These narratives are like worldviews, but more immediate—the stories we actively tell ourselves and each other about what's happening. While worldviews operate mostly below consciousness, deeply rooted and slow to change, narratives are alive and dynamic. They're constantly being shaped by what we take in and, in turn, they affect how we process new information. They're the front-of-mind stories that guide our responses to everything unfolding around us.

Narratives are like a pair of glasses we look through to make sense of things, and in a day and age when so much is shifting at such a rapid pace, many people's narratives about the world are discombobulated and up for review. Old stories about how the world works and our place in it are shifting. Old definitions of success and health have gone out the window. Our understanding of how to wield power is having a total make-over. It is like our narrative glasses are in need of new prescriptions! Or a different colored lens, a new frame shape... or maybe something totally different altogether (*spiritually-anointed, AI-powered contact lenses, maybe?!*).

As a development practitioner and changemaker, I regularly encounter wildly different narratives about the state of the world—everything from apocalyptic collapse to us living in a golden age of prosperity, international cooperation, and technology. I've met economists so convinced their evidence-based approach is the end-all-be-all that they snap back in contempt at anyone who questions it (*cough, cough—like yours truly*). I've met anarchists who shoplift from the local bodega with deluded self-righteousness, "Robin Hood style." And I've met people so certain "the other side" is at fault that they've cut ties with loved ones as a political action. Thanksgiving dinner? Hell no. Or if they go, it's only to do battle.

As I look around the world, I am constantly in a process of making sense of what I see. I do so from the lens of being a professional and forever-student of the world. I do so as a social creature who is embedded within networks and echo chambers that influence what I see. And I do so as a feeler and spiritualist who is attuned to the subtle energies below the surface of it all.

How we make sense of what we see and feel shapes the way we show up and respond. There is a difference between arriving at the conclusions "the world is inherently fucked up" and "there is big work to do." The latter has the potential to inspire creative social action. The former has the potential to lock someone up due to overwhelm—to spawn apathy, hopelessness, or complacency. All of this affects how we relate to the world and her pain.

In our age of information and interconnectivity, there is a line between using awareness to inspire action in pro-social ways, and having so much awareness of so many awful things that it paralyzes you. The narratives we form help us to walk this line.

Therefore, I'm of the humble belief, that we need narratives—even loosely threaded ones—that can help us dance with the reality of our times constructively. Narratives that help us be of service in the unique way we're called to do so. We need perspectives—even partially-baked ones—that offer new vantage points on what we're witnessing; that can help energy slide and glide when it gets stuck; that can breathe new life into dank, stagnant space. Especially when it comes to the world's pain. adrienne maree brown says "…all organizing is science fiction" [38] because changing the world requires us to imagine futures that don't yet exist. That's what narratives do: they create space for new possibilities when the present feels stuck.

This chapter introduces healing-centered narratives—lenses that don't deny the pain we're seeing but interpret it as meaningful, as a sign of movement, not just collapse. A signal that something in our system is speaking, and perhaps, that we're finally in a position to listen.

Before we go any further... what's it like to think about the narrative you use to make sense of the world? Thinking about them like a pair of glasses, take a moment to remove yours and hold them up to the light. What do you notice about them? How do they shape how you see the world?

A healing-centered lens on the world

One of the reasons why I launched We Heal For All is because there's this divine, restless nudge within me that keeps pushing me to look at our world as if she is a person. To take what we know about individual healing—in every sense—and apply to the collective to see what new insights it might offer.

There's a fractal-like quality to this exploration. If you're not familiar with them, fractals are self-repeating patterns that show up across nature. The branches of an oak tree, for instance, follow a fractal pattern, with each branch—as they get smaller and smaller—resembling the larger one in structure and design. The wisdom of fractals is also found in spiritual traditions. The Hermetic phrase "as above, so below" speaks to how different layers of reality mirror each other.[39]

When I use a healing-centered lens to look at the world, and take a fractal-like approach to do so, I find that new perspectives start to emerge—ones that help me find meaning in the world's pain in new ways, see our breakdowns as part of a larger process, and feel more equipped to respond.

So that's what we'll play with here. The three sections below will answer the question: "Why is the world in so much pain?" from a healing-centered lens. The answers take frameworks and principles from the healing-centered sciences to make sense of the social phenomena we see.

The three narratives we'll look at are:

» The world is in so much pain because…
» We are collectively awakening.
» We are resourced enough to heal.
» Our system is communicating with us about what needs to change.

We are collectively awakening

The first healing-centered perspective we'll explore is this:

> *The world is in so much pain because…*
>
> **We are collectively awakening. Our awareness of the world's pain goes hand-in-hand with this.**
>
> *Collective awakening puts us in greater touch with the world's pain. Feeling the world's pain is a natural byproduct of collective awakening and the expansion of our collective consciousness. We need to collectively do "shadow work." Our collective shadow comes into greater view as we collectively awaken.*

At first glance, when many of us hear the word "awakening," images of light and bliss often follow. Spiritual teachers have offered guidance throughout the ages on how spiritual awakening and the expansion of consciousness lead to greater freedom. As I tune into this freedom, a liberated spaciousness fills my body. The divine universe I am part of becomes ever more apparent. It is a homecoming. A holy sacredness of my place within it all.

However, there is also another side to awakening that is less frequently conjured up. It is the fact that with awakening—to new dimensions of consciousness, to new awareness of one's self, or to new ways of being—comes a journey that is not all light and love. It is a journey of trials and tribulations. A journey filled with resistance and confusing psychic debris, with grief and anger. The journey of spiritual awakening comes with pain, and with this pain comes the need to heal.

The global awakening of human consciousness has been explored by many great futurists and thinkers. However, popular culture's overemphasis on the light side of awakening has left many to abandon the idea that collective awakening is happening… or even possible. Look around. If the times we live in are supposed to reflect some sort of spiritual awakening for us as humanity, then we've got it all wrong!

But consciousness studies tell us that painful, mucky things are actually quite normal. The journey of spiritual development includes the need to reckon with the things that are not of service, as much as it is about welcoming in newfound gifts. Phases of contraction are critical to the larger rhythm of consciousness development. It is a journey of twists and turns, leaps and backslides.

From this point of view, it is as if we as a society are going through a collective awakening process. We are waking up to the way we work as a world; how we impact people and the planet, for better and for worse. The world's pain, and the collective responses born from it, are a byproduct of this. Each new news report, scientific article, and current event opens our eyes to new things in new ways, forcing our collective consciousness—and our shared morals, values, and worldviews—to stretch and pull in order to make sense and accommodate it.

No wonder there is so much division and discord. This process of collectively awakening is tender and raw, as this point in time isn't comparable to any other. Yes, we have experienced upheaval and breakdown in the past, but never with this level of conscious awareness. Never have we been able to track what is happening so closely, to understand it so systemically, or to feel its effects so viscerally.

The age of awareness has given us an expanded view of ourselves as a system. Things on the margins of our periphery are now in clearer view, and we are figuring out how to work with this newfound consciousness.

As we talked about in the previous section, the age of awareness is driven by advancements in media technology.[40] Advancements like this are at the heart of cultural and political changes throughout history. From the printing press in the 15th century, to newspapers in the 17th and 18th centuries, to radio and television in the 20th century, and now the Internet. Media revolutionizes the way we connect with each other; and how we exchange information and art. It's a key thing that shapes our collective consciousness.

There is a quote often attributed to English poet William Blake which goes, "*Culture is a totality of imaginative power.*"[41] And media technology, my friends, is at the heart of our collective imaginative power. How is this time of collective awakening shaping ours?

Let's look at the abolition movement of the 18th and 19th century. This was the movement within the United States and parts of Europe to abolish slavery and the Transatlantic slave trade. Before newspapers came onto the scene, information about the conditions within which enslaved people lived was limited. The explosion of cheap print and literacy changed that. The eyes of millions of ordinary people were opened to its horrific nature, shifting moral attitudes and politics around slavery. First-hand accounts from enslaved people reached the public like never before, allowing the movement to mobilize opinion and ultimately reshape the collective narrative.[42]

All of this change took time; it was bloody, and far from linear. There was violent pushback and resistance. Trial and error. Two steps forward and four steps back. However, chattel slavery as that period knew it was eventually abolished.

What's interesting to me here is the role that collective awakening played within this. How many eyes needed to be opened before things changed? When does a society reach the tipping point where enough minds and hearts have shifted that something becomes morally unacceptable?

Tying this to our current day and age, are there ways we can leverage our age of awareness to make the most of this moment of collective awakening? Spoiler alert on my take: yes! Through collective healing. But let's stay on this collective awakening point for a bit longer.

Seeing the world as something that's going through a collective awakening process gives me so much compassion for her. When I think about my own journey of awakening, the one I shared with you at the beginning, I'm reminded of how fucking scary it can be at times. Maybe you can relate? I find that anyone who's ever dipped a toe in the path of knowing one's self can attest to that.

There can be a lot of resistance that comes from awakening, and this is the case for the collective, too. Hilda Charlton, a spiritual teacher of mine who I love dearly, told this story in one of her classes at St. John's Cathedral of the Divine in New York City in the 1980s:

> *"The new untraveled paths sometimes seem fearful and uncomfortable... [T]hat very consciousness is what you have been working toward life after life. When it comes, it is a new consciousness, and you do not know how to use it. You get scared. We like the comfortable. It is like the story of the fisher lady, who is taken into the palace, and given a room filled with flowers, and she sniffed and said, "What is this horrible smell?" Flowers. She went out and slept with her fish. She was comfortable with the fish smell, but not comfortable with the palace flowers."*[43]

We get comfortable, right? Even when we "know" there's something wrong or something better for us.

For the collective, historical inaction on climate change comes to mind. Scientists have been ringing the alarm about global warming since the 1890s.[44] (*That's right... that's not a typo*). Psychologist and author Zhiwa Woodbury offers us the term "climate trauma" to understand why we've been so painfully slow to respond.[45] He argues that society's "dissociated unresponsiveness" to science's findings is a psychological defense mechanism. The climate crisis's existential threat makes us collectively shut down and go numb. The implications of what we know are too challenging to bear, therefore we can't handle it.

The collective defense mechanism Woodbury identifies is resistance within our long climate awakening. Despite 130 years of scientific reports and political campaigns, we've been unable to stabilize this awareness and act on it. The implications for our way of life—and the fears they triggered—were too much to process. Shifts in consciousness are often born from crisis. Record temperatures and extreme disasters have been necessary for climate awareness to finally take hold. The world's pain is part of this awakening process.

Across spiritual and personal development traditions, awakening includes contraction. As periods of expansion bring in new information, periods of contraction follow, as a person reckons with what they now see—reconciling contradictions, navigating confusion, grieving what's lost.

It requires healing everything that gets kicked up. As Ken Wilber put it, we need to "clean up" after we wake up.[46] That means doing shadow work—tending to old beliefs, unresolved pain, and confusing psychic material. Patterns that no longer serve become clearer—we can see them in contrast to what's now possible.

Within transformation, periods of contraction are equally as important as periods of expansion. Sure, the expansion part is fun. Ah-ha moments. Renewed energy. Clear insights and vision. Whereas the contraction part... forget about it! The need to face inner demons. To trek through the dark night of the soul.[47] It can make the best of us want to abandon ship.

However, as many spiritual teachers remind us, the darkest hours are right before dawn. Right around the corner of darkness lies a new round of light—with new insights, peace, connectedness, and love. The contraction prepares us to receive what's next. The shadow work helps awakening take root and builds our capacity to integrate what's new.

What if this is true at the collective level, too?

Because it's clear that as a society, we feel lost. Tender. Disoriented. It's as if we're in the midst of a collective dark night of the soul. The fear and overwhelm are real. However, from this perspective, they're not signs of failure. They're signs that something essential is underway.

As author, activist and evolutionary thought leader Duane Elgin puts it:

"Real change involves deep learning through direct experience. Great suffering is the evolutionary fire that awakens our compassion for ourselves, one another, and the world... The suffering, distress, and anguish of these times will become a purifying fire that burns through ancient prejudices and hostilities to cleanse the soul of our species."[48]

Shifts in consciousness are often born from crisis—and these are the times when the deepest, most lasting change can happen. We can hold this vision for the collective—not just to comfort ourselves, but to give direction about what to do.

If we are extensions of the collective, then that means we can be catalysts for her change—through our own consciousness. We can use what we're feeling as an entry point to do this work—to grapple with what's happening and unearth wisdom about what it means for our morals, values, and worldviews.

We have never been this self-aware as a system. We are the eyes of the world and are waking up with her, for her, and alongside her. Like a shaken-up snow globe, we can help guide where the floating pieces land, and help integrate the new types of consciousness that the world needs right now.

What's it like to see yourself as waking up alongside the world—being an extension of her collective awakening process? Where in your life do you feel the contraction side of this awakening process—experiences of resistance, grief, confusion as it relates to the world? Where do you feel the expansion side—possibility, hope, renewal?

We're resourced enough to heal

The second healing-centered perspective we'll explore is:

The world is in so much pain because…

**Our awareness of our collective wounds means
we are resourced enough to heal them.**

The fact that we feel the world's pain so keenly is because, we as a collective, are resourced enough to do so. The world's development has positioned us in a way that means that collective trauma is able to resurface. Enough of us have what we need for exiled parts of our collective consciousness to be seen, felt, processed, integrated, and—ultimately—healed.

As I continue exploring the world's pain through a healing lens, I arrive at collective trauma. Why does there seem to be so much of it now? And what does it mean?

There are so many collective wounds in our faces these days—they come in all shapes and sizes. There are some related to the present, like political breakdown or school shootings. Some are related to the future, like the takeover of AI or climate collapse. And there are some related to the past. We'll do a deep dive about collective wounds in chapter 11, but for our purposes here, when we talk about collective trauma, we're talking about collective wounds related to the past.

From where I'm standing, these wounds seem to be shouting at us to pay attention to them. We can see it in the rise of social unrest and the intense issues we face.

Trauma has entered society's zeitgeist over the last decade. To explore collective trauma, I need to lay some groundwork on what trauma is at the individual level, so we can apply what we know to the collective. Let's start there.

Healing-centered sciences teach us that trauma is any experience that is too much, too fast, or too soon for a person to process. Instead, the experience overwhelms them, and their nervous system turns to creative forms of self-protection to help them get through what they're experiencing.

When this happens, the protective mechanism pushes the emotional energy the person is feeling—the unbearable pain, shock, or horror—outside of their consciousness so they can regain stability. The anguish is out of sight and out of mind, if you will, helping the person get by. If the person doesn't have the tools to work with what they feel, that sidelined emotional energy gets stuck in their mind and body and turns into trauma.

These wounds end up remaining stuck and unprocessed until a person has what they need to work with them. This is often framed in terms of resources. Once the person has enough resources, inside and outside of themselves, for the trauma to feel safe enough to resurface, then they are able to work with that old material to help it heal.

As I use fractal-like thinking to consider how this might apply to the world, I'm filled with curiosity. Maybe the deep pangs of historical and collective trauma reverberating across the globe are here because, as a collective, we finally have enough resources for them to surface and be healed. Maybe the world's pain we're feeling is, at least in part, old traumatic material that we are now ready to face. Enough of us have what we need to do so. These exiled parts of our collective consciousness are making themselves known and asking to be healed.

Let's play with what we know about trauma to see what we see.

Trauma is born from our need to protect ourselves

Trauma forms when a person doesn't have what they need to process what they feel. Instead, they unconsciously or subconsciously turn to creative forms of self-protection to prevent themselves from feeling it.

These protective mechanisms are helpful by nature. They make it so we can keep going in the midst of crisis. If we didn't have them, we wouldn't be able to survive.

However, over time, especially once our circumstances have changed, these patterns of self-protection can begin to hold us back. They can lead us as individuals to feel anxious, depressed, and disconnected from ourselves and others.

Looking at our collective system from this perspective, it makes me wonder, in what ways is collective trauma keeping us stuck in patterns that are no longer helpful to society? What forms of protection made sense to the survival of society in the past, but no longer make sense today?

Did past generations have the tools they needed to process mass tragedy?[49] Were the people of Ireland able to process the devastation and hardships of the Great Famine of 1740? Did the families of soldiers during the American Civil War have what they needed to cope with what the conflict brought?

The answer, in part, is yes. Across time and cultures, our ancestors have had different ways of dealing with crisis. From community rituals to religious ceremonies, they had many wise practices designed to develop resilience and resistance that we can benefit from today.

On the other hand, though, we know that in the midst of dire circumstances, there is very little room to truly heal. When a group of people are in survival mode, all they can do is just try to survive. Our history is full of mass tragedies and harrowing periods that have required just that. From war to genocide to enslavement, epidemics, persecution… the list goes on. Therefore, it makes sense that our ancestors relied on creative forms of self-protection to survive. And thank goodness they did! Otherwise, we wouldn't be here.

The idea that there is unprocessed collective trauma in our system makes me think about two ways that trauma gets passed down and baked into society: intergenerationally and systemically.

Looking at intergenerational trauma, epigenetic research shows that unresolved trauma can be biologically passed down through our genes. Tragedy and hardship affect gene expression, and these changes can be inherited by future generations. The nature versus nurture debate around intergenerational trauma is a false binary, because both of these factors are at play. Beyond the biological component, protective patterns are socially passed down, shaping how family members see themselves and navigate the world. When intergenerational trauma stems from shared hardships like poverty, violence, or war, these patterns become reinforced by the wider community and can solidify into what we call culture.

Systemically, collective trauma shapes how societies are built and how they respond to crisis and change. Groups bearing this trauma build societies shaped by that pain, both consciously and unconsciously—influencing policy, education systems, military approaches, foreign relations, and more. These collective responses are most likely helpful and strategic for some time. But just like at an individual level, this can run its course and end up keeping the system stuck in patterns that are no longer in its best interest.

Collective trauma teacher Thomas Hübl describes it like this:

> "We might envision the impact of collective trauma, such as that created by the Holocaust, as a series of scars etched into the tissue of our shared humanity. Succeeding generations will enter the world bearing those scars, and it will be their task to integrate the psychological impact of whatever traumas created them."[50]

Trauma is stuck emotional energy in the form of exiled parts

Since emotions, at their core, are just energy, when overwhelming feelings get pushed to the side, they do not disappear, but instead get stuck in the person's mind and body and turn into trauma. This leaves a person tethered to wounds and unresolved material that have been exiled from their conscious view. These wounds instead live in the shadowy corners until they're ready to be healed.

This is where the concept of being "triggered" comes into play. Since the emotional energy is unresolved and won't go away on its own, when something activates or brushes up against that stuck energy, the person can be transported across space and time to the pain point's origins without being aware that it's happening. This can make a present-day incident feel much bigger than it is, as it doesn't just carry the present-day pain, but also all of the heartache from the past.

It makes me think of protests and pushback against mask mandates related to the COVID-19 pandemic. I remember a team-wide work meeting I went to in recent years where we were asked to wear a mask. It was the venue's policy, so the organizers asked us to do so.

For many of us, the request was no big deal. For others, it crossed a serious line. There were a handful of my colleagues who vehemently opposed having to wear a mask. Heated emails were exchanged, and the whole team was copied in, so we all witnessed what was going down. One person threatened to boycott the meeting altogether. Whispered confusion came from others, *"What's the big deal? Just wear the freaking mask!"*

What was perplexing to some people made total sense in the bodies of others. For my colleagues who were pushing back, it wasn't just about the masks. It was the historical wounds of authoritarianism and state control that the mask mandate held. The confinement and overreach. The lack of physical autonomy and threat of punishment. The request to wear a mask brushed up against wounds that were deeply held within my friends' bodies, which were made even more tender and outraged by being misunderstood.

Trauma's ability to transport us across space and time is rooted in the fact that the amygdala, the emotional epicenter of our brains, doesn't have a sense of chronological time. Instead, it operates on an amalgamation of perceptions, senses, concepts, and ideas that we have taken in throughout our lives *(and, I'd argue, beyond)*. These "trauma knots," as neuroscience educator Sarah Peyton calls them,[51] are part of the reason why trauma can be so confusing and disorienting, and why it can put us in touch with implicit memories and intrusive thoughts outside of our conscious control.

From this viewpoint, I can see the rise in social unrest and waves of political reckoning in recent years as an upheaval of traumatic memories coming to the surface. While we're grappling with urgent present-day issues—police violence, sexual misconduct, ongoing conflicts—these current crises also awaken deeper collective traumas from our past. It's this combination—today's pain activating yesterday's unhealed wounds—that fuels the intensity of our reckoning process. You can see it in the global wounds of white supremacy and racism through the Black Lives Matter movement. The centuries-old wounds of patriarchy and violence against the feminine through the #MeToo and LGBTQ+ movements.

When I look at the rise in social unrest and political upheaval from the lens of collective trauma, all I see are the wounds that underpin them. Wounds that are seeking to make themselves known, and now seem to have new ways to do so. They have new platforms or amplifiers with which to speak.

Does this rise in social unrest mean these injustices are getting worse? In some cases, absolutely—we're seeing real, urgent harms that demand immediate response. But when I zoom out and consider the progress we've made on justice, freedom, and safety—as imperfect as it is—I wonder if this unrest is also collective trauma surfacing. For many communities, this trauma isn't just historical—it's continuous, fueled by ongoing systemic violence. Current injustices don't just cause new wounds; they reopen old ones that never fully healed. Perhaps these movements have gained their momentum from both present-day urgency and centuries of unprocessed pain finally being heard. This isn't about choosing between attributing responses to current harm or historical trauma—it's about recognizing they're inseparable.

This brings me to the topic of resources.

Trauma resurfaces when we are resourced enough to heal

Trauma remains unprocessed until a person has the resources—internal and external—for the traumatic material to safely resurface. Once the proper conditions are in place, the wounds show themselves. Arriving at this place is a reflection of a person's development and their environment.

The term "resources" here refers to whether someone has what they need to work with the emotional material they feel. Do they have enough resources within their psychological, emotional, and spiritual capacities to handle a situation? Do they have the resources they need around them—in terms of safety, support, and accompaniment—to address disruption in their life?

Children are a great example of how internal resources affect trauma. Young children generally need support when it comes to regulating their emotions because their brains are still developing. This is why parents soothe crying babies, with the parent's nervous system serving as an auxiliary brain to help the child regulate. On top of that, children lack the cognitive frameworks they need to make sense of harrowing experiences. Without adequate adult support, they're especially vulnerable to trauma—they simply don't have the internal resources to process what they experience alone.

External resources refer to a person's environment and the type of support they have around them to help them to process what they feel. Is the person physically safe? Do they have the time and space to process what they feel? Most importantly, do they have emotionally safe people around them—or even one emotionally safe person—who can help carry their load and walk with them in what they are experiencing? Without external resources like these, emotional energy can quickly turn into trauma.

When I think about this with respect to the collective, the idea that a system needs to be resourced enough for trauma to resurface and heal shines a new light on the amount of collective trauma I see. It makes me think about the massive amount of economic development that the world has experienced in recent history. This economic development is undoubtedly causing serious problems, but it's also helping us to meet people's basic needs better than at any other point in history.

For instance, did you know that there are one billion fewer people in extreme poverty today compared to 1990?[52] One billion! This means one billion more people have access to basic human rights like clean drinking water and roads. This is huge—and it's just one of many things we've achieved as a global community.

In general, we are meeting people's basic, physical needs better than at any other point in history. Extreme poverty has plummeted, literacy rates are through the roof, and almost all children are vaccinated worldwide. Two hundred years ago, 80% of the world lived in extreme poverty—it was the standard way of life. By 1990, that had dropped to 36%. Today, it's just 10%.[53] Even with the global shock of COVID-19, extreme poverty continues to decrease, albeit at a slower rate.

It makes me wonder if the fact that we as a collective are so aware of the world's pain these days, and are going through wave after wave of reckonings, means that we are at a place where we have what we need to work with this emotional energy in new ways. Maybe these collective traumas feel safe enough to resurface in our collective consciousness: to show themselves to us more clearly in hopes of being healed.

This idea is fascinating! It feels like a breath of fresh air in the otherwise dank and stagnant place we're in as a society. Through this lens, our system may be arriving at a point in its own development where we as a collective have the capacity and environmental conditions we need to process and heal these wounds. We might think of this capacity in terms of technological development—mass media, information and communication devices, and the Internet. Alternatively, we could see it in terms of consciousness—cognitive bandwidth, psychological safety, creativity, and knowledge.

We are hurting as a world, and perhaps we're able to hurt in this way because we finally have the means—socioeconomic and cultural—for our collective past to more fully surface. We're able to feel those wounds with a new depth and in a new way because enough of us have moved beyond survival mode that we can access the intergenerational, historical, and systemic trauma stored in our collective consciousness for centuries. With more of us having basic safety nets—physical, social, economic—this unfinished business finally has airtime.

Drawing on Dr. Maria Bravehorse's framework for healing historical trauma,[54] this developmental milestone invites us to confront and understand the trauma held in our history in order to release and transcend it. Literature on post-traumatic growth highlights the positive personal and psychological outcomes that come from healing trauma.[55] It makes me think that this opportunity also exists for us as a collective.

Seeing the rise in collective wounds as a reflection of our system's development and strength helps me approach what is happening in the world with more compassion and a new understanding. The prevalence of our collective wounds, especially the collective trauma kind, helps me see opportunities. It gives me hope that we may be ready to heal the collective wounds we've inherited; the cultural ailments lurking in our communities; and the intergenerational skeletons that have been swept under our family rugs. We're ready to do so, not only to feel better as individuals, but also to be of service to the larger transformational process our world is undergoing.

Indigenous rights activist, spiritual teacher and transformational change-maker, Sherri Mitchell Weh'na Ha'mu Kwasset offers us this:

"…we must heal the wounds from the past. When we don't allow ourselves to acknowledge the pain, the deep agonizing soul pain that results from historical trauma, we aren't able to recognize that we all carry some measure of that pain within us. Instead, we allow it to isolate us and keep us cut off from one another. We also fail to recognize that the cause of that pain is not only a violation against us, it is also a violation against life itself… The wound that is causing the pain that we are now feeling as a society is not new. But how we respond to it can be. When properly addressed, this pain can mobilize us and lead us towards the transformation we so desperately need. If we can find the courage to face it openly and honestly, it will heal us." [56]

How does it feel to imagine the rise in collective wounds as a sign of developmental readiness and a chance to heal collective trauma? What becomes possible? What lands for you about this? What doesn't?

Our system is communicating something to us

The third healing-centered perspective we'll explore is:

The world is in so much pain because…

Our collective wounds are a way our system is communicating to us.

Our collective wounds are in our faces for a reason. The emotional energy they carry is information our system is communicating to us, to help us adapt. Therefore, our job is to learn how to listen and use it in constructive, positive ways.

The widespread rise of the world's pain makes many of us think we're going downhill—and in some ways, we are. But drawing from what we know about individual emotions, what else might this surge of emotional energy in our collective nervous system mean? How else might we understand it?

The topic of emotions is a big one. The good thing is that we know more about what they are and how they work than at any point in history. The challenge? We're up against some pretty rigid cultural taboos that make a lot us feel ashamed and confused about them.

However, emotions are key to our health and survival as humans. They're baked into us by eons of evolution. They show us what we need and drive us toward it. So I wonder: if emotions in my individual system are key to my health and evolution, then are emotions in our collective system key to society's health and evolution? And if so, what do we do with them?

Let's unpack what we know about emotions and see what we find.

Emotions have a purpose

Imagine this:

You're walking down a trail in the woods. You see a bear. You feel FEAR!

Before you're even aware of it, you take off running in the opposite direction, moving as fast as humanly possible. It's only once you're back at the parking lot, with no bear in sight, that you catch your breath and think, "Shit… that was scary…"

What just played out for you in this hypothetical bear story is your emotions going to work for you in the way they're designed to. Their purpose isn't to overwhelm and disorient us, but to help us respond to what's happening around us. They're foundational to the way our mind-body-system works.

Therefore, let's start here, at this baseline premise that emotions have a purpose to them that's key to our health and survival. This might sound like a trivial place to start, but in a world that still greatly misunderstands what emotions are, and instead encourages us to *shove them down*, it seems like a good starting point.

Extending this to our dear sweet world, it makes me think that the emotional energy circulating throughout our collective nervous system is also integral to her. It's no mistake that it's here. The collective anxiety, outrage, and confusion aren't things that need to be shoved down and ignored. Instead, they have a key role to play in our collective's health. This makes me curious about what that role might be, especially as it relates to society's evolution.

Why our collective evolution, you might ask. Because emotions are evolutionarily positioned to be of service to a system. For us as people, they drive us to respond and adapt to our environments in order to survive, and ideally thrive. Therefore, it would make sense that the emotional energy in our collective nervous system is here to do something similar, but for us as a society.

Each emotion has an intelligence to it based on its evolutionary purpose. Remember when you saw that bear and, without even thinking, were propelled to get the hell outta there as quickly as possible? That is the evolutionary intelligence of fear. It has an impulse to it (i.e. the impulse to run) that is based on its evolutionary purpose: to keep you safe and respond to danger.

Every core emotion[57] has its own version of this. Whether it's anger needing to protect or sadness needing comfort. Each one has its own intelligence and impulse based on its evolutionary purpose.

Expanding this to our collective system, the collective grief, rage, and confusion that is so palpable these days signal, to me, that we're in the midst of an evolutionary process of change. The presence of all of this emotional energy means that we as a system are being propelled towards something new; and that the purpose behind these intense, widespread feelings is to help us get there.

The evolutionary perspective helps me hold the collective outbursts and outcries as being part of a deeper, longer process. Instead of them being a sign of latent defectiveness, they actually reflect an inherent intelligence within our system that is coming to the surface to help us adapt.

They get us to move

Our core emotions are packed with key information about what we need and how best to respond. They're what psychologist and emotions educator Hilary Jacobs Handel calls "programs for action"[58] because they push us to do something—to run, fight, hide, or seek comfort—in response to what's happening.

Because emotions push us to take action, the intelligence of our emotions lives in the body. Thinking back to when you were on that hike, before you were even aware of it, your body—fueled by the intelligence of fear—changed states in order to run. Your blood flow moved from digestion towards your heart and lungs; your pupils dilated and your muscles engaged. The intelligence of your emotions kicked your body into gear before your mind even had a chance to process what was going on. It was only once you were out of harm's way, and had a moment to breathe, that your thinking brain could recognize the fear you felt.

Thinking about emotions in this way, I can see waves of emotional energy in our collective consciousness driving change and getting us to move. Driving people and institutions to respond and take action. Pushing people to take to the streets. Grabbing our institutions by the shoulders and urging them to change.

There's a degree of unconsciousness to the world's pain too. It arises from something deeper than the cognitive level or from logical sources that seek to drive action or social change. I'm thinking about climate change and anti-Black racism. Climate scientists have been sounding the alarm for over a century: reports and UN bodies and articles, but it didn't inspire action. This is similar to the call to see the depth of anti-Black racism within America's history.

What sparked the waves of racial reckoning that transpired in 2020? Yes, it was George Floyd's murder. Yes, it was the ability of media technology to transmit the video across minds and hearts in seconds. Yes, it was the fact that it was in the midst of the pandemic, when more people were home and glued to their phones, and already in a tender, vulnerable place. All of these factors contributed to the world being set on fire with awareness of anti-Black racism. But none of those factors existed in a vacuum. All of them were part of the system. They were who and how the system was in that precise moment. A culmination of forces and vectors that had been in play for decades, centuries... since time immemorial! All leading up to this one moment in time within our system's larger evolutionary process.

Once again, looking at this from the perspective of the world's pain, what ultimately drove the mass uprising and global protests? The emotional energy people felt within it all. It wasn't just learning facts and figures. It wasn't just objectively looking at rational information about the issue at hand. It was experiencing George Floyd's life being stolen from this Earth. The stealing of Black lives across time and space, going back to the slave trade when people were ripped from their homelands. Deep and wide wounds were able to come to the surface. They could use George Floyd's death, media technology, and the pandemic as a vehicle to make themselves known. The timing of it all—the system positioned just so, arranged precisely to allow these collective wounds to come through in the way they did.

Listening to collective emotions

Emotions reveal us to ourselves. This is one of my favorite ways to sum up what emotions do. They reveal to us what we need and when, what's good for us and what's not, what our values are and what's important to us, what we love and what we don't, and what we're drawn to and repelled by. They are meant to be allies in our life journeys, communicating insights and intuitions about our paths, if we know how to listen to them.

I'm compelled to think that this is the case for our world's emotions too. Instead of seeing them as a cacophony of noise that's here to overwhelm us, this view of emotions invites me to see them as allies to us in our collective path. They, too, are able to reveal important information about what we need and when, what's good for us and not, what our values are and what's important to us—but at a collective level.

From this view, the rise in heightened collective emotions is actually an intelligence in our system that's coming to the surface for us to work with. It's bubbling up because it has insights about what we collectively need. It contains information about how to adapt to our fast-changing world and how to respond to the times we live in. What a shift in perspective!

So then the question stands: how? If this is true, that the emotional energy in our collective system can be used in generative, informative ways, then how do we do it? How do we not let it overwhelm and overrun us, but instead learn to listen to it and harness its power?

This is where collective healing work, as I've come to know it, comes in. It's the practice of processing the emotional energy we feel, allowing it to reveal insights to us, and then bringing those insights into the world through the way we live our lives. (*We'll dive into this in depth in the next part*).

Looking at collective emotional energy this way is inspiring. It means we can shepherd this energy by giving it support and healthy outlets, rather than allowing it to get caught in old harmful cycles that further weigh us down with pain. We have an opportunity to do big, beautiful healing work right now. If we can work with this energy in constructive, powerful ways, we can use it to transform society—within ourselves, our families, our communities, our institutions, the media, and our policies.

What changes within you when you see collective emotions as intelligence trying to speak to us? How might this shift the way you approach what's happening in the world?

I'm taking a big breath here. Thank you for going in on all of those with me.

It's one thing to see this moment as a time of awakening, healing, or integration. To see spiritual purpose in breakdown. However, in my humble view, nice narratives aren't enough.

What does all of this mean for our lives? If we see this as a time of collective healing, then how do we do collective healing work... *in practice*? If we see this as a time of awakening or consciousness shifts, then how do we support those shifts... *in our lives*?

That's where we'll go next—into practice.

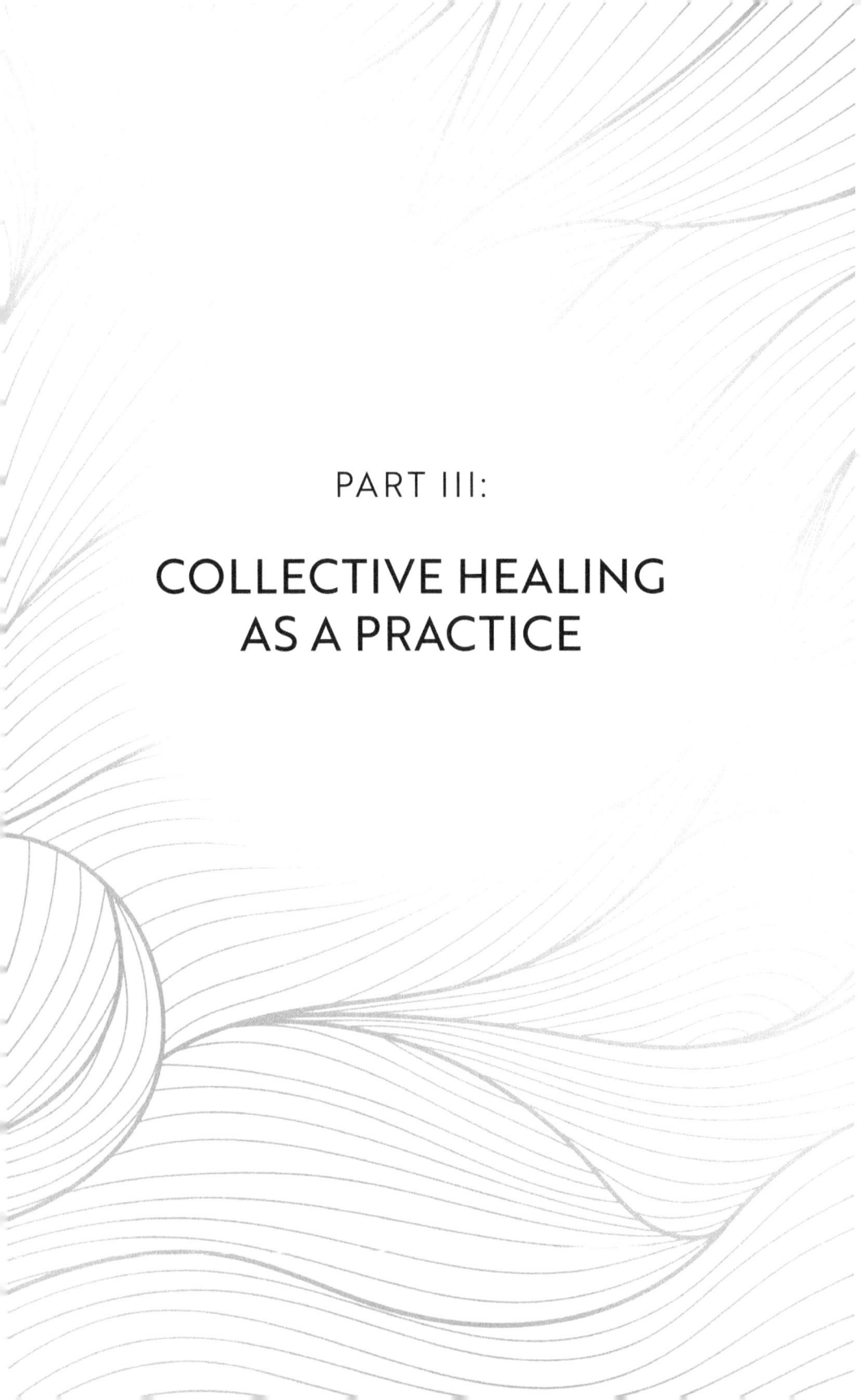

PART III:

COLLECTIVE HEALING
AS A PRACTICE

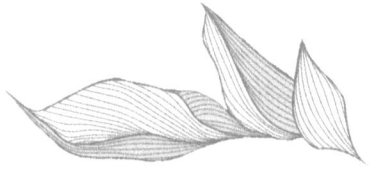

Chapter 5

HOW THE PRACTICE WORKS

So here we are, where the rubber meets the road—the practice section. Specifically, we'll explore the collective healing practice that's emerged through We Heal For All. This practice takes everything we're seeing and sensing about the world and works with it in soulful, healing-centered ways, helping us show up to these times and serve in the unique ways we're each called to.

If we were in a workshop setting together, I'd imagine we'd just returned from lunch. Everyone had an opportunity to get fresh air and feel the sun on their skin; to digest the morning and get a nice meal in their bellies. Conversations with kindred spirits fill the outskirts of the room, slowly winding down as everyone makes their way back to our shared space. They grab lemon water or an extra blanket as we settle in for the next part of the day.

As we've been discussing throughout this book, we have a new, more intimate relationship with the world—a world that's changing fast and in a lot of pain. Many of us feel overwhelmed and helpless because of it all. We pine for blissful ignorance and throw our hands in the air in a gesture of "what the fuck do I do?" We can end up shutting down and going numb, or furiously spinning our wheels and then spinning out—being all in one moment, and then needing to retreat the next. We don't know what to do with it all.

Our hearts are inextricably tied to the world and our desire to serve her. The issues we face are rooted in human suffering, death and loss, unfairness and injustice, and abuse. As changemakers, helpers, and healers, we're called to be of service precisely because of this pain—either from our firsthand experiences or because we experience it secondhand through our community and the world at large.

As a practice, collective healing recognizes the role your heart plays within all of this, and sees that as a key capacity to strengthen. The world affects all of us—the entirety of who we are, including the emotional, psychological, and spiritual dimensions. Collective healing supports these layers and understands that there's value in doing so.

The collective healing practice I share here offers a game plan and support system. It does so in a way that isn't just self-oriented, but that is rooted in an understanding of how this work feeds into the world—the shifts in our collective consciousness and the role we each play in helping it evolve. This practice is more than self-care (*although self-care is awesome*). It helps you unearth the wisdom held within what you feel—about your morals, shifting values, and existential questions in our complex age—and bring that into your life and the world. Yes, collective healing can help you feel better, which is worthwhile in itself, but it also keeps you stay connected to the larger collective body you're part of and the unique role you're meant to play within it.

We also live at time when we need to do things differently. The division and discord amongst us has to find a way to shift. This collective healing practice offers a way to engage with each other politically without getting stuck in ideology...or ideas at all. This might sound like a strange way to approach politics, but with our social fabric disintegrating like it is, we need new ways to meet each other in our shared humanity.

In the section below, we'll do the following:

» Look at what the collective healing practice is through a framework that guides you from feeling to action
» Explore three different ways this practice works
» Unpack the foundational DNA that runs through everything

In chapters 6 through 10 we'll do a deep dive into the guiding principles that will support you to carry out this practice in a community setting. However, for now, let's stay high-level and look at what this practice is all about.

COLLECTIVE HEALING
PRACTICE FRAMEWORK

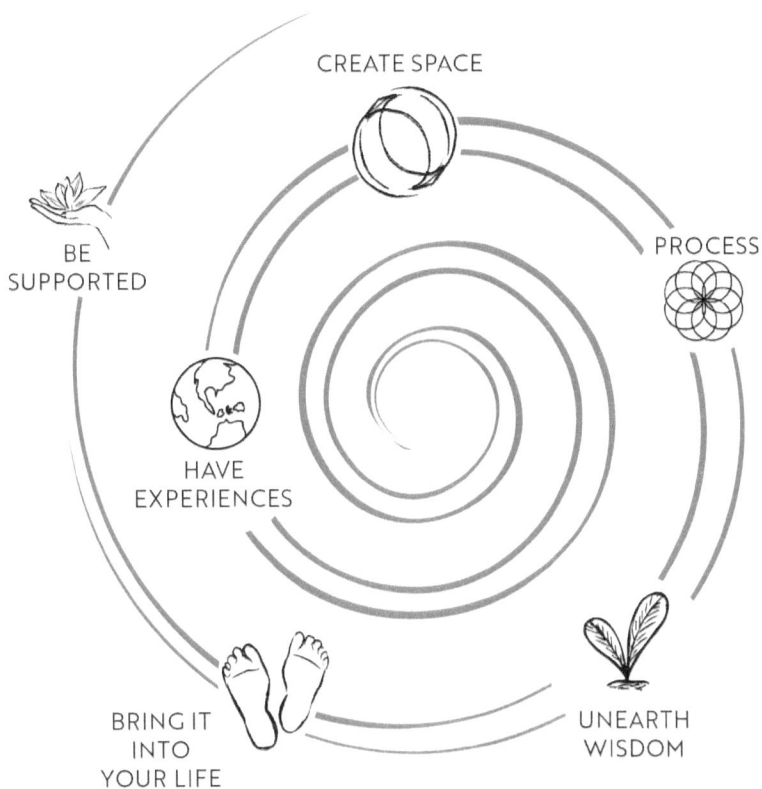

CREATE SPACE

PROCESS

BE
SUPPORTED

HAVE
EXPERIENCES

BRING IT
INTO
YOUR LIFE

UNEARTH
WISDOM

A high-level look at the practice

The collective healing practice follows a framework of five key steps that work together in an ongoing spiral:

1. **Create space.** *For what you're feeling and experiencing, current events and crises, and the questions you're holding and grappling with.*

2. **Process.** *Use healing-centered tools to help your emotions move in constructive ways.*

3. **Unearth wisdom.** *Receive guidance and wisdom from what you feel.*

4. **Bring it into your life.** *Put those insights into practice by integrating them into your life.*

5. **Be supported.** *In an ongoing fashion through community and more.*

While I call them "steps" for clarity, they're more like movements in an ongoing dance. They spiral rather than forming a straight line, building on each other in a continuous fashion.

The collective healing practice:

» **Is an ongoing spiral.** As new events occur and we have new experiences in life, we can turn to this practice to work with what we take in. All five steps—creating space, processing, unearthing wisdom, bringing it into your life, and being supported—all feed into one another, so the best way to think about it is as an ongoing spiral.

» **Can be done in a community or solo.** This collective healing practice is best done in a community setting or as something held between two or three people. The "collective" part of this practice is not merely tied to the fact that we're working with energy related to the world. There's an extra dose of magic that comes from practicing this in a community. That said, these steps can also be done on our own, and often need to be. We can't always be in Circle. There will be times when we'll need to turn to healing tools on our own, so what's presented here can be thought of in that way, as well.

» **Can be formal or informal.** We can think of this as a formal practice we engage in through a program, like a We Heal For All Circle series. Or we can think of this as something more prevailing and subtle—a map we hold in the back of our minds and turn to throughout life's journey. It can be an informal, ongoing practice that we're constantly engaged in to some degree.

The We Heal For All Circle model

While there are many ways to go about doing the collective healing practice, I want to share the specific model that has been my learning laboratory: my We Heal For All Circles. This Circle model is a concrete example of the practice—a way of bringing the framework to life in a community setting.

Everything I've learned about what supports collective healing—all the guiding principles I'll share in the coming chapters—has come from facilitating these Circles. They're where I've learned what supports transformation, what invites wisdom to come forward, and what gets in the way. They've been my testing ground for discovering which tools and approaches best serve each step of the framework.

By understanding how these Circles work, you'll see a path for implementing the practice while gaining insights you can adapt to your own context and community. These are ways to create a shared space where people can slow down, come into their bodies, feel what they're feeling, and share authentically. The goal is to create a place where we can come into our hearts and speak openly about our personal lived experiences with the issues, causes, topics, inner changes, outer realities, and work we care about deeply.

In my We Heal For All Circles—whether done in-person or online—we use meditation, storytelling, and resonance practice to process what's going on in the world and within ourselves. They're typically 90-minutes long and move through an arc:

> » Opening the Circle to ground and arrive,
> » Connecting with ourselves through meditation (or an embodiment practice, contemplation, mindful art, etc.),
> » Connecting with others through storytelling and resonance practice (which is what we spend the majority of our time doing),
> » Connect with that which is greater than ourselves (whatever that means to each of us) to offer the energy up and cool down,
> » Close the Circle with gratitude and good-byes.

This structure creates a container that's both spacious and structured—allowing deep sharing while maintaining boundaries that support everyone's process.

WE HEAL FOR ALL CIRCLE MODEL

Open Circle	Connect with Self	Connect with others	Connect Beyond	Close Circle
Arrive, ground, acknowledge	Meditation	Storytelling & resonance practice	Cool down & integrate	Gratitude & goodbyes

Throughout Circle, the two main tools we use to co-create a healing-centered space are:

1. **Guidelines for Listening and Sharing:** These serve as a community agreement that makes the space as constructive and supportive to as many as possible. Here we agree not to fix or save each other, but to practice accompanying each other in our experiences. See Appendix C for a sample of the agreements.

2. **Resonance practice:** This is where we keep our listening active and embodied. We wiggle our fingers or pat our hands over our hearts when we notice our own emotions or bodily sensations responding to what someone else is saying. This lets the person know, "I am right here with you," and keeps us grounded in our own practice of self-awareness and emotional mindfulness.

These two tools work in tandem: The guidelines create a container of safety and authentic relating, while resonance practice keeps that container alive and dynamic. Together, they transform a group of individuals into a field of shared presence—where wisdom can emerge not from any one person, but from the space in between us. You can read more about this in chapters 6 through 10.

Acknowledgment of influence

This type of practice isn't new, or even novel in some respects. The need to heal in community and to heal as a communal body has deep roots across history, cultures, and social movements. The practice of discovering and rediscovering our personal values as they relate to the world is as old as time. There are also loads of brilliant practitioners, artists, facilitators, and activists who offer different versions of this, who I am grateful to be in concert with, learning from their unique takes, and being part of this larger web of collective healing practices that exist out there.

What I share here builds on this time-tested invitation to figure out how to be in a relationship with the world, and the healing-centered tools—old and new—that can help us to do so. In this wide, interconnected world, the collective healing practice I share has been influenced by so much and so many. It's particularly influenced by the following:

» Women's circles and Indigenous ceremonial circles
» Emergent group processes, such as the Presencing Institute's Theory U
» Emotional healing and resonance practices, like those taught by Hilary Jacob Hendels, the AEDP Institute, and Sarah Peyton
» Buddhist-ecological practices, such as Joanna Macy's The Work That Reconnects
» Somatic and awareness-based practices, like the Pocket Project's Global Social Witnessing
» Movement training methods, such as Relational Uprising and Training for Change
» BIPOC, queer, feminist, disability justice-led collective liberation movements
» Contemplative spiritual practices, such as the Centering Prayer
» Trauma-informed social change teachings, such as Anneke Lucas's Unconditional Model
» Systemic Constellations and Family Systems Constellations

See Appendix D for a deeper dive into the larger field and lineage of collective healing.

Ways this practice works

There are three distinct yet overlapping ways this practice tends to meet people. You can think of these as different ways to go about doing this practice—different perspectives on what collective healing makes possible or offers us as practitioners, depending on where you are and what brings you to it. The three ways to think about it are to:

» Help us feel more resourced and steady in the face of everything we're holding—so we can show up more whole-heartedly in our lives and work.
» Use our personal experiences for collective consciousness shifts—understanding our lives as meaningful contributions to cultural change.
» Listen to the collective's voice—using our bodies, hearts, and emotions as tuning forks for the collective field, and letting the wisdom of the world speak through us.

Let's look at each of these.

Help us feel more resourced

One of the most immediate ways the collective healing practice meets us is by helping us feel more emotionally and relationally resourced in the face of all that's going on. For many, this is the entry point: the need to feel less overwhelmed, more grounded, and better able to navigate the intensity of these times. By creating space to process what we feel, collective healing supports our emotional well-being and our ability to engage more wholeheartedly.

The specific benefits of this are explored throughout the book. What's worth underlining here is that tending to what we feel is part of how we sustain ourselves and the work we do in the world.

Use our personal experiences for collective consciousness shifts

So often, it can feel like our personal experiences don't matter. It feels like the system is so big and far away from us that what we're experiencing on the ground—whether it's distress or trying to make a change—doesn't make a difference. This results in conversations about emotional support being very focused on just helping us to feel better about what's going on. It's an emphasis on personal wellness and self-care to stay resilient in the face of change.

Alternatively, in social change circles, emotions like grief or rage can sometimes be talked about as something we need to take care of to get back to work. *Process your grief so you don't burnout. Make space for your anger so you're not an asshole.* There is the sense that what we're feeling needs to be regulated and controlled so it doesn't get in the way of what we're trying to do.

From this point of view, our emotions are something that we need to deal with so we can get back to the "real" work of organizing, demonstrating, building a social enterprise, or whatever it might be. *"Take 'em out back behind the barn and deal with 'em!"* is the sentiment. Maybe you've come across this too?

However, I actually see something different in this work. While this line of thinking makes sense in some ways—unprocessed emotional energy takes a toll on our well-being and affects how we show up in the world—there are things that this outlook misses. The idea I want to invite you into here is that everything that gets kicked up for us about the state of the world isn't in the way of doing "the work," it's where a dimension of the work actually happens. Specifically, the dimension related to consciousness shifts.

When we talked about the collective consciousness, we saw that from a sociological perspective, it's where our collective sense of self resides: our shared morals, values, and beliefs. Well, what's happening for us on the ground—the anguish we feel around moral injuries, the confusion around existential questions—doesn't exist in a vacuum. Instead, it's directly connected to shifts going on in our collective consciousness. They are happening in parallel with each other.

We can think of ourselves as having a symbiotic relationship with the collective consciousness. Like we talked about earlier, it's an external phenomenon and something that lives beyond us, meaning it doesn't die when one of us dies. But even so, we also directly affect it by the way we live our lives—the morals and values we embody, and the worldviews we use to make sense of things all affect the collective consciousness. Yes, it can feel like an uphill battle as we swim against the tide. However, in this way, we are all constantly co-creating the collective consciousness and culture born from it together through our minds, bodies, and lives.

Because of this, there is an opportunity to be of service to shifts in the collective consciousness by working with our experiences on the ground. The emotions we feel about what's going on in the world are revealing to us the evolution of our morals and values. These shifts in morals and values are in lockstep with shifts in the collective. By grappling with the moral injuries and existential questions we're facing these days, we not only help ourselves, but also support the larger evolution of the collective.

Therefore, we can step into this collective healing practice with the intention of processing what we feel in order to be of service to these larger shifts. This perspective doesn't negate the need for emotional support or personal care—it expands on it. Yes, we tend to ourselves because we matter. And that care, when it is held with intention, also serves something larger than us.

Listen to the collective's voice

Another way we can approach this collective healing practice is by seeing it as an opportunity to listen to the world herself. We can use ourselves as antennae to tune into the collective's voice and listen for what she wants us to know.

This approach might make complete sense to some of you and be foreign and confusing to others. It brings us nose-to-nose with our own philosophical understanding of what emotions are, how they work, and how we as humans work more generally. Are we solely confined to the limits of our own mind and body? Are we inherently separate from the systems of people and life that we exist within? Or do we exist within a tapestry of interconnected webs that shape and form us? Are we actually in relationships with each other, the cosmos, and all of life in subtle, energetic ways that society's material worldview fails to help us recognize?

As a feeler, I'm of the mindset that many of us are able to empathically feel things that live beyond our own personal lives. I say "many of us" because there are your resident sociopaths or those of us who fall on the more stoic end of the emotionality spectrum for whom this is less accessible. But for the majority of us, especially my fellow feelers, we can empathically attune ourselves to other people and sense what they are feeling. I believe that this empathic ability extends beyond just people and includes our greater world.

Therefore, this collective healing practice can be used to allow the world to speak through us. Noticing what we notice within ourselves—what bodily sensations we feel, what impulses arise, or what images flash across our mind's eye—and using that as breadcrumbs for what the world is saying.

As Thomas Hübl puts it, "*The Collective Voice is archetypal and universal, and its message can be delivered to the group field through one or more people.*"[59] The world speaks through us. She is reflected in the media, in social phenomena, and in laws that are passed. She also speaks through our own personal lived experiences—through our own hearts.

When we watch news reports or see grotesque imbalances in the world around us, the feelings we feel are, in part, hers. There are layers of what we experience that are from the world. We are like antennae that pick up on her frequency. Each one of us is uniquely attuned to pick up on different parts of her.

We can develop our ability to identify this within ourselves and listen for the wisdom within those feelings. We can serve as a surrogate for the collective, in order to unearth the intelligence embedded within those feelings.

What is the anger I feel from the world saying? What needs to be protected? What lines have been crossed that need to be redressed? What new forms of boundaries need to be defined and asserted? How does that translate into community organizing or policy? How does that translate into my own lifestyle, relationships, work, and identity?

This way of listening may take time to develop, but it's a skill worth cultivating. When we learn to tune in to what the world is feeling through our own hearts, we begin to understand that we are not separate from her pain—nor her wisdom. The collective healing practice gives us a way to enter into this relationship and sense what wants to be heard.

Reading through these three ways of engaging with the practice, which one speaks to you the most? Which one resonates deeply? And which doesn't or does less so?

The foundational DNA

Before we get into the guiding principles in the next five chapters, I want to lay out the foundational DNA of this practice. You can think of these as the essential building blocks that run through every part of the practice.

The collective healing practice is:

- » Healing-centered
- » Co-creative
- » Awareness-based
- » Feminine
- » Trauma-informed

Healing-centered

Collective healing is healing-centered, which may sound obvious at first, but the term "healing-centered" has a specific meaning within the fields of psychology and neuroscience.

Healing-centered practices—in psychotherapy or coaching—work with emotions as the main entry point for transformation, as opposed to a person's thoughts or behaviors.[60] Because of this, these modalities—especially the ones with a growing evidence base—offer us a wealth of knowledge about what emotions are, the neurobiology of them, their evolutionary purpose, and how to work with them in practice. This body of research and clinical work underpins the collective healing practice I share with you here.

Let me give you an example of how this plays out:

Let's say you're scrolling through news about families being separated due to mass deportations and suddenly feel overwhelmed by a wave of grief and helplessness. The conventional response might be to analyze why this particular event triggered you, or to remind yourself to "focus on what you can control" and move on.

A healing-centered approach would invite you to actually feel that grief fully—to slow down, notice where it lives in your body, and listen to what it might be telling you. Maybe that grief is pointing you toward how deeply you value human dignity and the family unit, or showing you your views about borders or law and order, or revealing beliefs about human rights and belonging that you want to live more fully. Maybe the helplessness is showing you a deep desire to be of service in some way you haven't considered yet.

Healing-centered work trusts that emotions have intelligence baked into them and, when given the right conditions to do so, they naturally reveal insights and guidance. Transformation happens through our emotions. They're our inner guidance system, evolved over millions of years to help us adapt to change and navigate life.

See Appendix E for a deeper dive into what the healing-centered sciences teach us about emotions and the Change Triangle, a practical map for navigating emotions developed by Hilary Jacobs Hendel.

Co-creative

Co-creating wisdom in a community setting is a cornerstone of this collective healing practice. These practices operate on the belief that none of us has all the answers, but all of us have wisdom to offer. At the center of this methodology is the belief that we come together not to teach or be taught, but to explore, witness, and co-create something new—especially in response to questions that don't have clear answers.

Co-creative approaches rest on the belief that there is wisdom within the group—that it can be tapped into and brought forward. It's a participatory process in which new insight or meaning emerges—not from any one person's brilliance, but from the interaction between everyone. It's not about pushing an idea forward. It's about listening with enough presence that something new can come through.

Approaches like this offer a counterbalance to top-down models of power. They take a more horizontal and relational approach, where everyone in the room is both teacher and learner. This shift is gaining traction across systems change work and within institutions like the United Nations, where the focus is moving towards creating the conditions for collective intelligence to come through.[61]

The co-creative nature of this practice also shapes the dynamics within a group setting. How do we come together in ways that feel generative and soulful? How do we tend to the energy of a community space so that it grows, deepens, and inspires rather than flattens or fades? Co-creative approaches help cultivate this kind of aliveness.

Awareness-based

Awareness, or presence, is at the heart of the collective healing practice. The practice invites us to cultivate an awareness of ourselves and our personal lived experiences as an entry point for personal and collective transformation.

Awareness-based practices help us to cultivate the kind of self-awareness that healing needs. They invite us to slow down and work with our thoughts, feelings, and sensations from a place of compassion and non-judgment. Instead of rushing to fix what we see, we learn to observe what is asking to be healed. We meet it gently, with space and attention.

Presence offers a contrarian antidote to the world's urgency. Instead of pushing forward to figure everything out—to do, do, do—we instead soften and slow ourselves down in order to sense. To sense what is happening—within ourselves, within each other, and within the world at large—and practice moving from there.

Within the collective healing practice, awareness can be found at the heart of things like:

> » Emotional mindfulness: What am I feeling? What do I notice within my emotional landscape right now?
> » Embodiment: What sensations do I notice in my body? What is my body like, right now?
> » Self-awareness: An ongoing understanding of my personal history, disposition, growth edges. Having context to make sense of what I feel and what it means for my role as a conduit for change.

Cultivating presence serves as an entry point through which we can listen to our own system's intelligence—and also a doorway for listening to the collective's. Not to rise above or transcend it, but to meet it in a way that helps it heal.

Feminine

The collective healing practice is feminine in nature—archetypally speaking. "Feminine," in this context, has nothing to do with gender. Instead, it refers to a set of qualities that are found across time, culture, and nature.

In archetypal language, the Feminine and Masculine are two energetic currents that complement each other. The Masculine tends to emphasize structure, logic, and action. The Feminine brings presence, feeling, and flow. Both are essential and exist within us. Yet in much of the world—especially industrialized societies—Masculine qualities are overemphasized, while the Feminine is undervalued or ignored.

The collective healing practice balances this by rooting facilitation and leadership approaches in Feminine qualities, such as:

» Experiential: The Feminine isn't focused on ideas—instead it invites us into our direct, personal lived experiences. The emphasis here is on process, not outcomes—allowing ourselves to slow down, tune into what's happening, and experience things beat-by-beat.

» Story-based: Rather than aiming for linear arguments or rigid definitions, the Feminine leans into stories—personal, relational, and collective—as a way of knowing. Symbols and metaphors within stories allow us to get closer to truth in nonlinear, layered ways. They spiral instead of stacking. Like many Indigenous oral traditions, stories plant seeds within a person's consciousness that bloom through reflection and lived experience over time.

» Ecological: The Feminine is inherently relational. It reflects the interconnectedness of life, like in ecosystems where every organism shapes and affects each other. It's also cyclical—honoring birth, death, decay, and regeneration as natural rhythms of transformation. In the same way, healing doesn't follow a straight line. It moves in cycles, and the Feminine holds that wisdom.

Trauma-informed

Recognizing the reality of trauma and supporting it the best we can is a central piece of this collective healing practice. Trauma is an inherent part of our world and—without making an assumption about you, dear reader—a part of most of our lives. This understanding is baked into the We Heal For All collective healing practice and woven throughout the guiding principles in the next few chapters.

Far from seeing trauma as something that's destined to hold us back, the healing-centered sciences offer us loads of tools for how best to work with trauma. This helps trauma to be understood and supported in its healing journey, rather than staying in the shadowy background.

Trauma, whether personal or collective, comes in many forms, and manifests for people in different ways. Being trauma-informed isn't a promise that a specific practice will heal someone's trauma or be the right fit for what they need. Instead, it understands the impact of trauma and integrates approaches within it that are sensitive and supportive of that.

Guiding principles: bringing the framework to life

Now that we've looked at the collective healing practice framework and the foundational DNA that runs through everything, it's time to get practical. How do we actually *do* this work? What supports each step of the framework so it can do what we hope it will do?

In the next five chapters, we'll dive deeply into exactly that. We'll look at each step of the framework—Create Space, Process, Unearth Wisdom, Bring It Into Your Life, and Be Supported—and unpack the guiding principles I've found most helpful. This isn't a checklist or a step-by-step facilitation manual (*that's what my We Heal For All Circle training is for*). Instead, they're ideas and approaches that help create the conditions—within and between us—for something transformational to emerge. They come from years of facilitating Circles, learning what supports collective healing and what gets in the way.

These principles are designed to help you—whether as a facilitator or participant—cultivate the kind of space where open sharing, connection, and insight about the times we live in naturally arise. The list isn't exhaustive, but they're the ones I've found to be essential to my collective healing work. My hope is that you approach them as something to be explored and tried on to see what fits, take home what resonates and leave the rest behind.

While the principles focus on group settings, there are some that equally apply to solo practice. I've noted where these adaptations fit.

Here's an overview of what I'll be sharing:

Create Space   Process   Unearth Wisdom   Bring it into your life   Be Supported

Create Space

Define the space

Arrive, intentionally

Co-create the container

Process

Ground before you open

Cultivate safety

Commit to each other's right to belong

Invite in the body

Move from presence

Process, together

Unearth Wisdom

See emotions as doorways

Trust what comes through

Designed for shared wisdom

Learn through shapeshifting

Bring It Into Your Life

First, integrate

Weave it into your life

Take an inside-out approach

Be Supported

In this, together
Change is ongoing; so is this practice
Embedded in something greater

*As a helper, healer, and changemaker, my guess is that
you're doing some version of this work already.*

*Maybe you've been honing inner skills to navigate these times that feel really
grounded. Maybe you're the person who naturally holds space when friends
need to process what's happening—in the world or in their lives. Maybe
you lead a group or support people directly in a similar way to my Circles.*

*Before diving into what I've learned, take a moment to recall
what you already know. Looking at this framework, where do
you see yourself? What tools, techniques, or approaches have
you discovered that feel juicy, effective, life-giving?*

*Take a few minutes to jot those down or connect with them. My hope
is that this next section supports you as you build on what you're
already doing. Like a tapestry, weaving your threads of wisdom
with what resonates here to create something even richer.*

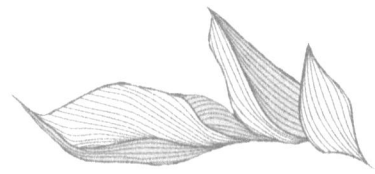

Chapter 6

CREATE SPACE

GUIDING PRINCIPLES:

Create intentional space for what you're feeling and experiencing, current events and crises, and the questions you're holding and grappling with.

> » Define the space
> » Arrive, intentionally
> » Ground before you open
> » Co-create the container

Create Space   Process   Unearth Wisdom   Bring it into your life   Be Supported

All this news bombarding the public without a healthy outlet is bad news bears. It's like being punched in the face and told to shut up. Like, no, I'm gonna say ouch, damn it. – Ethan, school teacher

We're all being affected by the world in new ways. We're inundated with information and media to the point of overwhelm. We are face-to-face with big, scary, and often confusing topics with no healthy outlet to say "ouch," as Circle participant Ethan put it. The world is hard to handle. It puts many of us in a position in which it's difficult to stand up for what we believe in or—in some cases—to even know what to believe in in the first place.

Not only that, but we also live in a fast-paced, production-oriented society that pushes us to go, go, go and do, do, do. Even if we understand the value of slowing down, doing it in practice requires us to go against the grain of mainstream life and the many internal patterns we've inherited because of it. Throw emotions or spiritual needs into the mix and the cultural argument to do so becomes even harder.

However, the understanding here is that if we don't create intentional space to feel and process the world's pain then that emotional energy gets stuck in our system. It doesn't just go away. We end up buried in layers of undigested energy—both our own and the world's.

Think back to times when you didn't have the proper time or space to process what you felt about the world. Maybe you watched a devastating video of what's happening in Gaza, or read another I-can't-believe-this headline about what's happening in DC. What did that do to you? Perhaps you got grouchier, snapping at people more easily. Lost motivation for whatever you were doing. Shut down and went inward, disconnecting from those around you. Or couldn't focus because your mind was racing. All of these are normal responses to unprocessed emotional energy.

Energy like this needs space, which is why the first step in our spiral-like collective healing practice is to do exactly that: create intentional space for what you feel, so you can work with it constructively.

Before I share the methods that have been most helpful to me, what about you? What comes up for you when you think about "creating space" for the world's pain? If you have any experience doing this for yourself or others, what principles of practice have you found most essential?

Define the space

Think about the last time you watched a live debate. Maybe it was during a presidential election or a video on YouTube of one progressive battling 20 Trump supporters. Better yet, have you ever been part of a debate club, let's say, in high school?

Whether as participant or spectator, there's a particular energy that you feel when you're in that kind of space. Your mind sharpens and your body tenses. Especially as a debater, the environment requires you to be on edge, instinctively prepping your next move.

This is because in a space like this, the goal is to outmaneuver each other, to win and prove a point. The atmosphere calls for something specific: quick thinking, defensiveness, and adrenaline.

Now, in contrast, think about a time when you were some place sacred. I'm personally thinking about a Hare Krishna ashram I visited in West Virginia or the huge, gorgeous Cathedral of St. John the Divine in Upper Manhattan. Maybe for you, a beloved synagogue comes to mind, or an Indigenous ceremonial site.

The air feels different in these places. The sounds are softer, the movements slower. Even if you don't personally follow the religious or spiritual traditions, spaces like these tend to evoke a certain response from us. Your breath may deepen, your shoulders relax. You may become more contemplative.

This is because spaces don't just exist in a neutral sense; they also shape us. They call forth certain qualities from us. How the space is designed—and, specifically, defined—does this. Which is why it's the first principle in this collective healing practice: define the space.

Defining the purpose of a space shapes both the tangible structure of things, as well as the unspoken atmosphere. Both of these things guide how people show up. It helps people know what the space is and isn't, and therefore what they can expect.

For instance, the Circle space I offer is first and foremost a place to process what is going on in the world. It is not a place to discuss ideas or brainstorm solutions about what to do. It is intentionally designed to complement the opportunities we have to educate ourselves and take action on issues.

In Circle, you won't learn a particular ideological theory, method for saving the world, or tools for taking action (*although you may hear them reflected in other people's stories*). It's an opportunity to balance the work each of us is doing in the world by creating space for the emotional, psychological and spiritual dimensions of our experiences; that place within us where our inner world meets the outer one.

This definition of the space's purpose is then carried out through all aspects of the Circle's design—from the Guidelines for Listening and Sharing to the reflection prompts to the opening introduction I give at the start of things. It serves as a basis from which the tangible aspects of the Circle come from.

Staying with our example of a debate, one of the things we agree to practice together in Circle—as outlined in the Guidelines for Listening and Sharing—is to not debate each other. Debating ideas is great, and much needed, but Circles are dedicated to being a space that revolves around the feelings underneath the ideas, not the ideas themselves. When we debate or critique each other's ideas, we relate to each other from the intelligence of the mind, and can easily get caught up in a layer of the human experience (*stories and political narratives*) that keep us at a distance. Circle is an opportunity to practice relating to each other from the intelligence of the heart, and to co-learn through the wisdom contained within what we feel.

This Guideline then infuses itself into the environment. Once it has been explicitly stated, it becomes part of the fabric between us. It invites each of us to practice staying in a place of nonjudgment and healing-centered listening, supported by other tools like resonance practice. The concrete Guideline is there to reference in case someone does slip into debating mode, but over time, especially when the same group practices together, it's something that becomes second-nature to the space, and the way we are when we're in it.

Solo Practice

It is rarely possible for us to drop everything we are doing and create space to process emotions. Instead, the invitation is to do so later and to let your mind, body, and heart know that. In the heat of feeling strong feelings about the world, see if you can turn to that part of you (*I see you*), validate what it is feeling and offer yourself some warmth (*you make sense*), and let that part know that you will create time for it later (*I got you*).

Then, when you are able to, pull out your journal, light a candle, pour yourself a cup of tea, and create space for what you experienced and are experiencing. Make carving out dedicated time a practice in and of itself.

Arrive, intentionally

A friend of mine—let's call her Abby—works as an Assistant Director at a global humanitarian organization that provides services to refugees. Her days are nonstop, to say the least. A blur of logistics and last-minute crises—things constantly coming up that needed to be done yesterday. She's always on the clock due to her team being spread across time zones.

As a result, she's always moving—between tasks, conversations, and decisions. So, when she came to her first Circle and was invited to slow down, it was really hard for her. Intellectually, she knew the value of doing it—and truly wanted to—but when it came to actually doing it, it's like she just couldn't.

If you're like me, Abby's experience is so freaking relatable. We live in a world that prioritizes speed and efficiency and getting things done. This is true across industrialized societies, and is especially true for those of us in under-funded sectors—nonprofit, education, social work.

We become so used to constantly moving that slowing down becomes foreign. Which is why, in Circle, we make a point to not rush in, but instead help ourselves arrive with ease. That is why it's our next principle: arrive, intentionally.

Imagine a snow globe or a jar of water with dirt that's been shaken up. All the particles swirling around and ricocheting off each other, moving at a particular speed. When held still, the particles don't just settle right away. They need time to slow down and reorient.

We are the same. When we step into Circle, our thoughts, emotions, and energy systems are moving in a particular way. Maybe we just put the kids to bed or sent off a last minute email. We carry energy and mental residue from what we were just doing, which is why making space to arrive is a core principle of this collective healing practice.

Having time dedicated to this at the outset is key. We can't expect ourselves to immediately drop in and change states. Instead, we create space to arrive—to let the ripples settle, and to transition into the space through things like the opening welcome, a round of warm up shares, and an opening meditation.

For instance, this can look like having buffer time at the beginning of the Circle for people to check in with themselves and see if there's anything they need that would make them even 5% more comfortable. A warm blanket? A glass of water? Closing the door or closing out computer apps that might distract them? We use this as a first gentle self-awareness practice that invites them to check in with themselves and see what they need.

I'll often use my voice and body language to support people to arrive. I slow down my tone, naming the fact that I'm taking a breath to cue to myself that we're beginning. I invite others to do the same.

An opening round of shares can be such a nice way to help people arrive, too. I like to keep these warm-up shares light, especially if it's a new group. Eco-Buddhist teacher Joanna Macy's The Work That Reconnects offers the prompt, "What's one thing you love about being alive on planet Earth these days?"[62] I find it so lovely. It's gentle and easy to answer. It brings people closer to their hearts. It doesn't plunge them into a convoluted, deep question about life's mysteries. (We'll save that for the big shares! *wink*). Instead, it lightly walks them in the direction of where we're going.

Slowing down like this is harder for some people than others. We are all up against cultural waters that push us in the opposite direction, especially as it relates to the world's pain. Additionally, trauma responses can keep some people in a fast-moving state in order to protect them from the unbearable pain they are carrying.

Hold the invitation to slow down with exquisite compassion and an awareness of these things. Explicitly name that it is okay if you cannot slow down. What does your body want to do? What would make you feel even the tiniest bit more supported? Don't be alarmed if someone needs to get up from the Circle to move, get water, or just leave.

Circle offers the gift of time—to allow people to arrive at the pace they need. The invitation is to create the conditions for it to happen—on its own time, in its own way.

Solo Practice

Once you create space for yourself, what might slowing down within your personal practice look like? It might look like taking a few rounds of nice, deep breaths. Or maybe you check in with yourself—is there some way to create more privacy? To feel safer in your space? Maybe you need to shake out your arms, legs, and body to rid yourself of excess energy.

Over time, you'll come to learn what things best support you to slow down and create space for yourself. It will undoubtedly be a moving target, but that's why it's a practice. It helps you move and dance with what you are experiencing in the moment, and learn from it for your larger journey.

Ground before you open

Before we open ourselves up—to the parts of us that want support or to each other—we need something solid to stand on. In this practice, that something is a grounded connection to your own body and heart.

Without it, it's easy to lose ourselves in the presence of others—to get caught up in what we think we should say or how we think we should show up. When this happens, we miss an opportunity to do true soul-level connection work. That's why grounding before you open is a core principle of this practice.

This step is about resourcing ourselves before engaging. It helps ensure that what we bring forward comes from a place of rooted presence, rather than reactivity, disconnection, or performance.

A spiritual teacher of mine, Ron Young, once said that in his meditation retreats, he always works from the base up. He starts with the basics of the practice—as a way to firm up the foundations for those who are familiar, and to make sure those who are new have what they need. This way, we all rise up together. That spirit applies here too—we begin by grounding, so that even the most hesitant or tender parts of us are included and can come along for the ride.

It's like tending to your home base before inviting in company—the company of other people's energies, and the company of different parts of yourself. In practice, this often looks like an opening meditation or guided practice that helps people connect with themselves before the storytelling portion of Circle begins. It builds on the work of arriving intentionally, deepening that inward connection before opening up to what's moving inside or between us.

When we ground before we open, we create the conditions for real presence. We begin to notice what is stirring within us, anchor ourselves in a well-resourced way, and make space for whatever is ready to be felt.

These practices help us:

» Move towards mindful observation. *How does my body feel in this moment? What's my mind like? What's present in my emotional landscape?* This invites you into a mindfulness practice, to notice what you notice from a place of curiosity and compassion. Observing how you are in this unique moment. Not trying to fix or change anything. Merely taking it in as interesting information.

» See what needs support. *What's alive for me right now that needs space? What within me wants to be seen, heard, and supported?* This opportunity to check in can inform what you share during the storytelling portion.

» Establish a baseline. *How am I, right now?* You can return to this place of self-connection again and again—as you listen, as you notice resonance, and as you share from a place of truth. It becomes a reference point to help you notice what shifts or changes within you throughout the practice.

» Take care of ourselves. *What do I need? Can I sense my feet rooted on the ground? Am I getting overwhelmed? Do I need a break?* Establishing this self-connection from the outset helps you answer these questions.

Since this collective healing practice is about the intelligence of the heart, I'll often facilitate a meditation that supports people as they move from the mind into their hearts. It can be helpful to bring the body into the mix, offering movement that releases excess energy or helps ground energy down and inward.

Throughout all these meditative practices that invite people to slow down, it is of utmost importance to give a lot of choice. Trauma can make slowing down feel really unsafe for some. I'll refer to it as "veto power." I remind people that if at any point I offer something that does not feel right for them, they have full veto power to swat it away. That applies now, during the meditation, and throughout the entirety of Circle (*and beyond*).

Solo Practice

The principle of grounding before you open applies equally within a solo practice. What supports you to feel grounded in your body? How do you know when you're ungrounded? What signals—in your mind and body—tell you that you need additional support?

Part of this principle is making sure you are well-resourced before you open yourself to emotional energy. It is also about recognizing when you need additional support, if you touch upon a nerve that's too challenging to hold on your own.

Co-create the container

The social field—have you heard of it?

Some call it the "social field," others the "relational field." Otto Scharmer and Dr. Eva Pomeroy from the Presencing Institute describe it as the invisible yet deeply felt energy that arises when a group gathers.[63] It's like a tapestry of energy or connective tissue that influences how a group moves, interacts, and works together—something that's alive in the space between us, that we are always shaping and being shaped by.

In Western culture, the social field is often unacknowledged or goes unnoticed. Because it is unseen, it is easy to assume that a space is just a space—that the way people interact, listen, share, or exercise power within a group setting is random or inevitable.

However, in Indigenous traditions, spiritual communities, and deep relational work, there is the understanding that the social field is a real thing and that it is something that can be—and needs to be—tended to. When we don't acknowledge or intentionally shape the social field, it doesn't just disappear; instead, the default setting of cultural dynamics—such as hierarchies, social norms, power imbalances—will step in to fill the space.

Think of a time when you stepped into a group setting and felt tension in the air, even before anyone spoke. Maybe it was a work meeting where the energy felt stiff. Maybe it was a dinner party where certain people dominated the conversation and others shrank into the background. No one explicitly said what the group dynamic would be—it emerged on its own. The design of the space—such as whether all employees were invited to speak—and the way people engaged (or didn't) set a tone and shaped what took place.

That's the social field at play. It is not neutral. It is shaped by the intentions, presence, and engagement of each person in the room. And when we don't recognize it, or assume the way things are just the way they are, we lose an opportunity. We lose the chance to shape the energy of a community space consciously, and to co-create it in alignment with our goals, which is why it's the next principle in our collective healing practice.

In Circle, we don't leave the social field up to chance. We acknowledge that how we each show up affects the whole, and that we are constantly co-creating the space, whether we mean to or not.

For me as the facilitator, a first step in doing so is that I name all of this at the outset. I specifically acknowledge that everyone's presence affects the Circle. Each Circle is beautifully different, and the way we each show up—what we're carrying and how we carry it—is what shapes that.

One of the most effective ways we intentionally shape the social field is through the Guidelines for Listening and Sharing. It's a community agreement and set of shared practices that guide how we relate to each other while in Circle. These agreements aren't here to police behavior, but to give structure to the social field that we're all building.

As a set of relational practices, the Guidelines for Listening and Sharing ask, "How do we want to be in relationship with each other in this community setting? What are we practicing together as a group, such as approaches to listening or nonjudgment?"

Reading the Guidelines is an opportunity to create scaffolding that shapes the community container, and therefore guides how things will unfold. For instance, members can agree to take their intention to share and to listen with compassion seriously. "*Nothing that is shared is unimportant or stupid. I do not make "you and us" statements, criticize, control, or dominate.*" Explicitly saying this can help each person feel a little bit more comfortable to share. If criticism does arise, the group can turn to the agreement as a source of support to get back on track.

I like to hold the Guidelines as a living, breathing set of practices, as opposed to a concrete list of rules. At the beginning of a program, or when a new group meets for the first time, I'll spend extra time on the community agreement and use it as an opportunity to co-create the container together—to see if anything needs to be added or amended. If we are meeting on an ongoing basis, I like to send out the list to everyone after the first Circle and encourage them to come back to it time and again, and to offer changes or amendments as new needs arise.

The more a community container can be co-created, the stronger and healthier it will be. For me, as the facilitator, this includes checking myself to make sure I'm not taking up too much space or pushing an ego-driven idea of what the space should be. It also looks like checking in with the group as I go, allowing pregnant pauses to give people an opportunity to chime in (*"How does all of this feel?"*), validating and integrating what is offered up into the flow of things.

This type of practice is helpful for any type of healing-centered group work. It is especially relevant to collective healing because there is an opportunity to engage in relational practices that embody and reflect what the group hopes to see more of in the world. The community space itself can become a radical act of resistance or a countercultural movement.

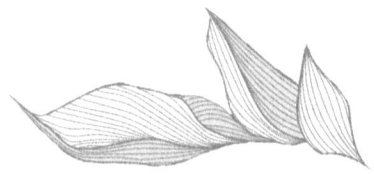

Chapter 7

PROCESS

GUIDING PRINCIPLES:

Process what's alive. Use healing-centered tools to help your emotions move in constructive ways.

>> Cultivate safety
>> Invite in the body
>> Move from presence
>> Commit to each other's right to belong
>> Process, together

Create Space · Process · Unearth Wisdom · Bring it into your life · Be Supported

have never encountered a space to openly speak about ecological grief in a supportive way. I left the space feeling so much lighter and comforted." – Cailin, city planner

Now that we've created the container for our work, we turn to the heart of the practice: processing what's alive within us.

The many complicated feelings we have about the world affect us. They can unconsciously drive us to do things we don't want to do—like stay up until 3am or yell at your uncle at Thanksgiving dinner. They can shut us down and make us feel hopeless. They can spin us out and drive us crazy. More generally, unprocessed emotional energy makes us unwell and unable to show up in the way we want to.

This is why, once you've created space for what you feel, the invitation is to process it.

By processing what's alive for you—feelings, questions, moral tension, inconsistencies, existential stuff—you help that energy move. What we know about the neurobiology of emotions is that, at their core, emotions are just energy. Energy, just like in physics, can't be pushed away or destroyed. It needs to be supported to move. Because if we don't, and instead block or suppress it, then that energy gets all backed up and leads us to anxiety, depression, stuckness, or collapse.[64]

In Circle, a lot of the processing work takes place during the storytelling portion. We do two rounds of equally-timed shares that give each of us dedicated space to express what we're feeling. For some, this becomes a story with a clear beginning, middle, and end; for others, it's streams of consciousness rippling out in non-linear fashion; and for others, it's wordlessness—pure expression through gestures, sobs, and song.

We process by sharing what is happening for each of us individually, and we also process by empathically listening to and resonating with the stories from others. It is a collective experience of holding and being held. Of supporting and being supported.

By processing what's alive for us, we help the emotional energy live out its full wave and reveal what the healing-centered sciences call the adaptive tendencies held within the emotions—AKA "the gold."[65]

However, before we get to the gold (see Chapter 8: Unearth Wisdom), let's take a look at what principles best support processing emotions within the context of collective healing.

Same prompt as before, but now applied to process. What principles of practice do you find most helpful for processing emotional energy—for personal purposes or for collective healing? Perhaps think of specific tools or techniques that help you move and work with emotional energy. What things work best for you or your community? None of this is one-size-fits-all, so tapping into your unique wisdom around this is key.

Cultivate safety

Let's be real: opening up to others about how we feel is hard—especially when it comes to the state of the world. With the level of intensity and urgency surrounding these topics, there is nothing that feels safe about it. There's the risk of being shut down, misunderstood, kicked out, or losing relationships.

Sharing our more vulnerable parts can leave us open to being hurt. It exposes us to judgment, poking and prodding or backlash. However, it's also where the juiciest revelations and deepest wisdom emerge—through safe, authentic relating.

The importance of safety—when it comes to healing, self-development, and trauma—has gained traction in recent years. This is a good thing, because we know from clinical psychology that emotional and psychological safety are key to healing. Emotions need to feel safe enough to express themselves. If they don't, they go into hiding.

But the promise of "safety" within a group setting can lead many of us to feel skeptical. Seeing a group advertise itself as being "safe" can feel like being lured into a lion's den. "*Come. Open yourself up to your most fragile parts… We won't bite…*" Yikes! Many of us instinctively snap back, "*You don't know me! How are you gonna pretend to know what makes me feel safe?!*"

This pushback make sense. Safety is deeply personal and subjective—what feels safe for one person might not feel safe for another. Not only that but safety, in the truest sense, is something that is earned over time. It comes from being in an ongoing relationship with someone. It's not something that's promised from the outset by a stranger. Feeling safe enough to let down your guard, especially the guards that protect your most vulnerable parts, requires time and trust.

Having said that, there are certain things we know that help emotions feel comfortable enough to surface and be shared. One cornerstone of healing-centered practices is what the AEDP community calls "undoing aloneness"[66] and what neuroscience educator Sarah Peyton calls "accompaniment."[67] Emotions need to be met with a certain presence and relational warmth in order to feel seen and understood.

Shame and aloneness are so often at the heart of what keeps us disconnected from what we feel. Many of us learned a long time ago that it's not okay to feel what we feel. We were left alone with our emotions and had to develop really creative ways to deal with them that, over a long period of time, have become unhealthy.

This is where resonance practice—or embodied empathy—comes into Circle.

Resonance practice is when we wiggle our fingers or gently pat our hand over our hearts when we hear something in what someone else is sharing that moves us. It's something we relate to, or something that "pings" and "dings" familiarity within our own emotional landscape. We silently let them know that we can relate through small, physical gestures. This simple act of physically reflecting back when we feel what another person is sharing is the ultimate practice of undoing aloneness within Circle.

It validates the emotion that the person is sharing, something key to helping emotional energy move in a constructive way. It lets someone know: *I am right there with you. I see you, I hear you, and I have not left you in the face of what you just shared.* It's the proverbial finger snaps, and helps create the conditions for emotions to feel safe enough to express themselves.

What about safety for the listeners? What do we do if someone gets triggered or deeply upset by what they hear someone else share? How do we cultivate any semblance of safety for them and their needs?

Luckily, resonance practice offers us a tool for that, too. It invites us into an ongoing practice of self-awareness, helping us answer: *how is what I'm hearing affecting my body, my heart, my inner world? What is it bringing up in me?*

This connection with self is paired with an explicit invitation for everyone to take care of themselves throughout the Circle. If you need to get up and move, to step out and leave, or to grab water—you are wholeheartedly, unequivocally welcome to. This commitment—to tend to ourselves and give ourselves what we need—is foundational, and something I encourage as a facilitator, and as a community, we trust each other to do.

The Guidelines for Listening and Sharing are also designed to help emotions feel safe enough to surface. One of the ways we do this is by resisting the urge to fix or save each other through unsolicited advice or feedback. This means that after someone shares during the storytelling portion, we agree not to jump in and try to give them advice or tell them what we think they should do.

While the impulse to help someone is often well-intentioned, offering advice without being asked can carry unspoken assumptions about the other person's experience. Instead of feeling supported, this runs the risk of making them feel misunderstood, dismissed, or even shut down. In Circle, we trust that each person has what they need. And if they don't, we trust that they will ask for it.

Cultivating safety in collective healing work isn't about eliminating risk—it's about creating the conditions where trust can grow, where vulnerability is supported, and where each person has the agency to care for themselves. When we cultivate this kind of space together, we make it possible for emotions to surface and to move in constructive, healing-centered ways.

Solo Practice

Learning to "undo aloneness" within ourselves starts with a fundamental shift: treating our emotions as valid messengers rather than inconveniences to overcome. When strong feelings arise—especially about the world's pain—we often abandon ourselves through judgment, telling ourselves we're being "too sensitive" or "too much." But what if we approached these feelings differently? What if we became the warm, steady presence we need?

This means offering ourselves the same compassion we'd give a friend who was struggling. When anger rises, we can acknowledge it without shame. When grief overwhelms, we can hold space for it without rushing toward resolution. This practice of self-accompaniment—meeting ourselves exactly where we are with warmth rather than judgment—creates an internal sense of safety. We become our own emotionally safe other, capable of witnessing and validating our full emotional range without abandoning ourselves when things come up.

Invite in the body

Have you ever had one of those moments when you suddenly remember you have a body?

Maybe you've been staring at a screen for hours, sucked down a rabbit hole of weird Reddit posts or locked in on a never-ending work task, and then, all of a sudden, you notice your jaw is clenched and you're practically holding your breath.

It's easy for this to happen, to be moving through life disconnected from our bodies. Our logic-driven, digital world prioritizes the intellect of the mind. The body is often seen as second-tier—primal and wild. Something that can be tamed and overridden.

But our bodies aren't second-tier, not by a long shot. They are our home bases, and the source of so much wisdom and information. Our bodies' intelligence is far-reaching, and that's specifically relevant here because emotions live in the body. This is why the next principle in our collective healing practice is to invite the body into the mix.

When you boil it down, each emotion is really just a bundle of physiological responses happening in the body. As an evolutionary tool, core emotions (anger, sadness, joy, excitement, disgust, sexual excitement, and fear) drive us to *do* something—to run, fight, throw up, repel, get big, pull close. This drive—and the energy behind it—is physical in nature. It gets us to act.

This is why, as much as we might try, we can't think our way out of having an emotion. Sure, we can zoom out and intellectualize our way through what we feel. This might help for the time being. Mental gymnastics can keep our feelings at bay for a period, but ultimately they won't offer relief. At the end of the day, because emotions live in the body, we need to *feel* them to actually get anywhere.

Emotions have a wave-like rhythm to their expression. They rise, peak, and fall just like ocean waves. They have a natural drive towards their own completion, meaning they want to live out their full wave and give us insights into our needs and environment. If we do not allow them to do that, though, and instead block or suppress them, then that energy gets all backed up and leads us to anxiety, depression, stuckness, or collapse.

Working with the physical and subtle experiences in our bodies is integral to emotional processing. Embodiment practices like this invite us to gently rest our attention on our somatic landscape, develop a better sense of this dimension of ourselves, and move from there.

In Circle, embodiment practices are woven in at every step: the opening meditation grounds us and invites self-connection; resonance practice helps us track our emotional responses in real time by noticing what arises in our bodies; the closing meditation allows us to discharge and release what needs to be let go.

Our bodies act as tuning forks for the emotional energy in the world. When we tune into sensations in our body, we can use those sensations as a trail of bread crumbs to figure out what we are feeling, or what we're sensing from the world. "*Oh, I feel a heaviness in my chest. Hm, this feels like sadness.*"

Coming down into the body can be hard, and understandably so. Being in our bodies is challenging for many of us, especially if we're carrying a lot of heavy unprocessed energy. It can also feel unsafe, often because it is. The title of Bessel van der Kolk's best-selling book *The Body Keeps the Score* sums up the role that the body plays in trauma healing.[68] Therefore, deep trauma requires specialized support to make the body a safe place to work with.

Keeping this in mind when inviting people into their bodies is paramount. You can do so by giving a lot of choices and options, underscoring each person's agency and right to not do anything you offer up. (*Think back to the "veto power"*). Cue several options—eyes open or closed or at a soft gaze. Also keep an eye out for times when someone seems to be getting overwhelmed to the point that they need additional support. Have trauma specialists or therapists on hand that you can offer them if they'd like. (*Low-cost options are great to have too!*)

Solo Practice

When it comes to doing collective healing work as a personal practice, bringing your body into the mix is so helpful. You can come to learn the unique ways that different emotions feel and show up in your body.

Climate anxiety and overwhelm, for instance, might manifest as pressure in your chest, tightness in your jaw, or pain in your back and neck—like the literal weight of the world sitting heavy on you. When you notice these, try some hearty audible exhales to help it move. Take a deep breath in and sigh out what you're holding, letting your breath carry away the tension. Roll your neck side-to-side, releasing whatever collective stress has lodged in your body.

Processing collective anger, on the other hand, requires more active discharge. When rage about injustice builds up, you might scream into a pillow or take a warrior stance—legs in a squat, fists raised, kicking and punching the air. Let out a warrior's cry. Imagine yourself confronting the leaders and systems causing harm.

Different emotions call for different things. The key is figuring out what works for you and making a practice out of doing it for yourself.

Move from presence

"Circle work is counter cultural… Emotional presence is at the forefront. It feels like we're speaking a different language. A language that doesn't have words." – Patrick, yoga teacher and coach

In a world moving at breakneck speed, we're carrying energies we don't yet have words for—collective grief that hasn't been named, systemic rage that has no outlet, nascent hope we're afraid to feel. These formless energies need space to find their shape. Which is why our next principle is to move from a place of presence.

So often, when we come into conversations or group settings, we have what we want to share rehearsed. We have a story lined up in the back of our minds. There are talking points that dictate what we can and can't say.

The issue with that is: 1) it puts us in our heads, which means we're in not our hearts and bodies—where our emotions and wisdom live. And 2) we miss an opportunity to allow the tender or less well-known parts of us to be heard. Energies that are new to us, so understandably don't have a set narrative to be expressed through. Energies that are overwhelming so need to just be spit out and cried through tears in order to be untangled.

This is why in Circle, the invitation is to allow rehearsed, mentally-controlled narratives to slip away, and instead step into a space within yourself where you move from presence. Concretely, this happens in the storytelling portion of Circle, where we give ourselves the opportunity to put words to what we feel; to put form to formlessness. When I introduce this part of things, I like to emphasize that these "stories" don't need to be clean-cut, with a clear beginning, middle, and end. Our stories don't even need to have words. The practice is to tune into the subtle energy present with each of us—pain, intuition, longing, outrage—and speak, move, emote, and make noises from there.

One thing that helps people practice moving from a place of presence, as opposed to being in their heads, is not having a set talking order during storytelling. Instead, when the floor is open, everyone is welcome to sense into if it's their turn to share. Do they feel called to speak in that moment? Is there something bubbling underneath the surface for them, ready to have its turn?

This means there are times when we sit together in silence, listening to the space in between us. Listening to the space within ourselves—our hearts, minds, and bodies—and also to the space that lives between us as a collective group. Sensing the subtle shifts and movements alive in that space.

When we do begin to put form to formlessness—words to what we're feeling—something magical happens. Emotions like to be named. It's like what was once amorphous emotional energy now has form. It has a placeholder to land in and relax. It is seen. It is understood. It makes sense.

Solo Practice

A beautiful way to practice moving from presence on your own is by free-form journaling or drawing. Allow yourself to slow down, come into your body, and support any critical thoughts to quiet. From there, write or draw from pure stream of consciousness. Don't worry what comes through—no one will ever see it. Use it as a practice to notice when your mind pops up and jumps in versus when you're creating from a different place—from intuition, emotion, and subtle energy.

Commit to each other's right to belong

"I had a healing experience sitting among a diverse group of individuals who all share the same sentiment of world peace. I think the future depends on groups like this one—sitting and discussing uncomfortable conversations, collectively— so that no one feels lost, left behind, forgotten." – Lauren, entrepreneur

There is such a fear of not belonging in our collective consciousness these days. A fear of being on the "wrong side of history," of saying the wrong thing, of not being politically correct or culturally competent enough. Of not being "enough" to qualify to be part of a certain group. My bisexual friend comes to mind—she told me she was trying to figure out how to "support the LGBTQ+ community," as if she stood outside it. She'd unconsciously removed herself from her own community because she didn't feel radical enough to belong.

Then there was my Black-Dominican-Polish friend who turned to me, a white person of European descent, for feedback on whether he's using the right anti-racist language. In my own confused attempts to position myself, I threw it back at him, "Please tell *me* if I'm not using the right language." We both sweated.

I share these vignettes to point to the anxiety so many of us feel around how to be good, socially conscious humans these days. Especially in progressive circles, there is a "skating on thin ice" feeling that persists around belonging. There is the lingering threat of being kicked out, which feels counterintuitive to a political camp that advances inclusivity.

This is why a central question in this collective healing practice is how to support divergence—how to hold diversity of thought, opinion, and feeling. It's important to do so to support emotions to heal—so they feel safe enough to be seen—but it's also important because it reflects reality. We live in a diverse, multidimensional world. We need different views and experiences to be whole. Diversity is the richness of life and is a reflection of any healthy ecosystem.

This is where resonance practice comes in handy. I described earlier how it serves the storyteller—undoing aloneness and reintegrating them back into the group when they're vulnerable. Resonance practice also serves the listener. It builds emotional mindfulness, helping us notice when our own emotions or bodily sensations respond to what another person shares. These responses might be empathy and recognition, or they might be disagreement and dissent.

When practicing resonance, the invitation is to stay curious when something stirs something in us that doesn't align—to stay open and ask ourselves why. When it's our turn, we unpack our experience using "I" statements, avoiding cross-talk or debate. We assume positive intention from others, and if something crosses a line, we speak our truth by naming our needs and boundaries rather than attacking.

Healing-centered spaces can get a reputation for forced harmony—where success means everyone agrees and stays "high-vibe." When conflict arises, people assume something went wrong. But that's a mistake.

We need to build our capacity for divergence—both in healing spaces and in everyday life. This requires a different kind of trust. Not trust that we'll all agree or that everything will be "kumbaya," but trust that we can disagree and still belong. Trust that we won't leave each other in the midst of that difference, instead knowing that the container can hold divergence because we have the relational and somatic tools to do so—resonance practice and the Guidelines for Listening and Sharing.

Resonance practice keeps us aware of our own emotional responses while listening to others. Even when someone's story triggers us or doesn't make sense, we can try to listen below the surface. What collective wounds are they expressing? Can we relate to the energy underneath their words, even if we can't relate to the story itself?

The Guidelines for Listening and Sharing serve as a tool that can explicitly define boundaries that the group seeks to practice. Not debating or domineering each other. Not trying to fix or save each other. These can serve as concrete things to look out for and fall back on if dynamics within the group start to go sideways.

There are times when divergent spaces aren't appropriate—when someone or a group are emotionally raw and in need of space that offers a more consistent view. This often takes the form of identity-specific spaces, where people can relax into knowing that they don't need to explain certain things or worry about harmful ideas coming up. There is a shared sense of the larger issue, especially if it's related to specific racial, cultural, or ethnic experiences —like being a transgender athlete, being Arab-American after 9/11, or being a Black woman in academia.

Process, together

As I've been sharing throughout this book, the term "collective healing" for me speaks to the need to heal collectively-shared experiences as it relates to our changing world.

There's another way that the word "collective" comes into play, though, specifically in the practice of collective healing. It's the role that the group plays in helping energy move and be processed.

I had always known this—that group work was a powerful way to heal. Nevertheless, I remember understanding this in a new way at a Circle early on when I was piloting the We Heal For All Circle model through a climate activist organization.

When it was time to share, an older woman with curly gray hair in her late 60s began to speak about her homeland. Being from the Pacific Northwest, she spoke about how the forest she grew up running around in, the trees that made up her home, has all been changing. Commercialism and forest fires over the past few decades meant that certain parts have completely disappeared.

The grief in her story was palpable, not only in her words but in her whole body. I hadn't come into Circle that night feeling grief. I was in more of a daze, dizzy with confusion about the state of things. However, her words took me somewhere else—somewhere I didn't know I needed to go, though once I got there, I was glad I had. It dropped me down into my body, landing me heavily in my chest. It gently cracked open my heart, a part of it that had been longing to be touched. Tiny tears welled up in my eyes.

I looked around and saw I wasn't the only one. People were nodding, with hands over their hearts, and a few eyes were misty like mine. Her sharing her story wasn't meant just to help her. It was also meant to help all of us, even if we didn't know it when she first began.

This beautiful memory reminds me of the power of hearing someone else's story, and—in the case of processing emotional energy—how helpful it can be to process our own. Even if we don't relate to the specific details of what they're saying, it can touch things within us that are universal and that exist beyond the superficial. For instance, I grew up in Central Pennsylvania, not the Pacific Northwest; I was in my late 20s at the time, not my late 60s. But that didn't matter.

Often times, emotions are thought of as something individually contained. What we feel is internal and personal—mine and mine alone. However, emotions don't exist in a vacuum. Instead, they exist in relationship with other people. The presence of the group itself shapes how emotions move. Depending on how it is held and co-created, a group can amplify emotions, validate them, or make them easier to process. What might feel overwhelming alone can be metabolized in the presence of others.

Many emotions—like grief, fear, or shame—are intensified by isolation. But when they are witnessed and received by others, they soften and shift. Seeing someone else express an emotion can normalize it within us, giving unspoken permission for our own emotions to surface. Sometimes, just being in the presence of someone feeling deeply is enough to move something within us.

Especially in an environment where we are invited to practice resonance with one another, we can cultivate the ability to meet each other below the surface of story and help the energy within it move. In a setting like this, when someone shares and then others wiggle their fingers or pat their hands over their hearts in resonance—communicating that "*I get you... I feel you...*"—the energy within the story is moved between us. The collective body of the group helps hold and digest what arises.

We don't always need to be the one sharing to be transformed—sometimes just listening wholeheartedly to someone else's experience can shift something in us. The way we feel is shaped by who we're with, how they hold space, and the larger collective field we're part of. Emotions move through and between us, shaped by the relational container we share.

There's a beautiful paradox that happens in Circle. Each person comes into the space with their own experiences, perspectives, and emotional truths, and we intentionally just talk about our own personal lived experiences. Yet we tap into something larger when we do. We access universal themes and shared energies that live beyond our own personal experiences and that connect us to the larger tapestry of life we're all part of and connect through.

Chapter 8

UNEARTH WISDOM

GUIDING PRINCIPLES:

Unearth wisdom. Receive guidance and wisdom from what you feel.

- » See emotions as doorways
- » Trust what comes through
- » Designed for shared wisdom
- » Learn through shapeshifting

Unearth
Wisdom

This big, wild, ever-changing world we live in leaves many of us lost. We don't know what to do or how to be. With so many options, choices, noise, and opinions bombarding us all the time, it can be hard to discern what's true and hear our own inner guidance about what to do.

This is why, once we've processed what we feel, and helped that energy constructively move, we arrive at an opportunity to unearth wisdom within it all. We can access the adaptive tendencies or intelligence held within them. What are our emotions telling us about our needs? What spiritual vision or moral clarity is buried in the disorientation? How am I being guided to live my values and show up at this time?

When we work with our personal experiences in healing-centered ways, we can receive guidance. We can receive clarity and support that we can put into practice and bring into our lives. However, before we get to the "application" part of things, let's drill down on this part of the process—unearthing wisdom.

Guiding principles that help support this leg of the process are:

- » See emotions as doorways
- » Trust what comes through
- » Designed for shared wisdom
- » Learn through shapeshifting

Unearthing wisdom—what does this phrase mean to you? When do you find you are able to best connect with the wisdom within you or the wisdom held within these times? What conditions best serve this?

See emotions as doorways

Are you familiar with mythologist Michael Meade? Among other things, he teaches about the Three Layers of Life, an archetypal template that can be found across cultural stories and myths.[69] We can think of these three layers as being dimensions of consciousness that we—as individuals or a society—can be in at any given time.

The first layer is the world of daily life. Think of this as the surface layer of things. It is the realm of "normalcy," where facts, common courtesy, and ordinary expectations dictate life. It is the world as it appears to be, shiny and put together, until it begins to crack. This brings us to the second layer.

The second layer is where dysfunction and upheaval live. It is where we encounter the shadows of life—anxiety, fear, and grief . If the first layer is what lives on the surface, the second layer is what has been hidden and buried just beneath it.

Beyond the second layer is the third: the realm of Universal Love, deep wisdom, interconnectedness, and grace. This is the layer of Awakening. The still point at the center of it all where the Individual Soul makes contact with the Soul of the World.

Meade argues that, collectively, these days, the cracks within the first layer are everywhere, leaving us squarely in the second layer, with the possibility of making greater connection with the third. What was once considered commonplace—institutional norms, cultural values, agreed-upon facts—has been breaking down. When these cracks appear, we don't just see the fractures, we feel them. As they widen, we more fully slip into the second layer.

When we are in the second layer, though, the third layer—the one of Awakening and soul connection—is nearby. We can more readily access it. Within this ancient template, we are taught that we don't get to wisdom without going through the layer of struggle. The grief and fear aren't in the way; they *are* the way.

This principle—that our emotions are doorways to wisdom—is core to collective healing. Emotions are often treated as something we need to control and regulate in order to keep moving or get back to work. But, as the Three Layers of Life teaches us, if we want to access deeper wisdom—about ourselves and the world—we have to be willing to feel.

What's beautiful here is that the healing-centered sciences say the exact same thing. Like we discussed earlier, our emotions are evolutionarily baked into us. Their purpose is to help us thrive and survive. They show us what we need and when we need it, what's good for us and what's bad, and how our environment affects us.

They are "programs for action," as emotions educator Hilary Jacobs Hendel says,[70] which is why they live in the body and get us to move. Anger rises to defend. Fear sharpens our awareness of risk. Grief slows us down, calling us inward. This is what's called the "adaptive tendency" of each emotion. The gold or insights held within what we feel that are meant to help us respond to what's going on around us.

In this way, emotions reveal us to ourselves—our needs and values. They serve as an entry point through which we can listen to our own system's intelligence, and act as a doorway for listening to the collective's. They can guide us in times of confusion, outrage, and overwhelm, especially in the face of constant mental analysis.

When we fully allow ourselves to feel an emotion, it shows us something we need to know. When strong emotional energy is safely discharged—whether through movement, breath, or another outlet—we can bring our thinking brain back online and assess what the situation calls for. What is the emotion revealing about the political crisis, the cultural breakdown, or the moment at hand? How does it shape the way you understand yourself and the things you need to be of service to; your role within it all?

Circling back to anger, its evolutionary purpose is to defend and protect (*think back to Mama Bear*). The way this shows up is in its impulse to fight. When we're angry, we want to fight. Understanding this, we can teach ourselves to notice when this impulse arises—"*Oh wow, I want to punch this person in the face.*"—and discern what this emotion is trying to tell us—"*I clearly need to protect some sort of boundary.*"

This is the intelligence of our emotions. It's communicating something to us that we need to know. The only way to hear it is by allowing ourselves to feel what we're feeling. Did the white hot anger you felt give you new insight into the type of advocacy you need to do or lifestyle choices you need to make? Did your boundaries around certain relationships or forms of work get clearer to you in some way? Has a part of you softened, now seeing a situation from a new perspective that offers you greater compassion and humility?

Nonviolent Communication (NVC), developed by Marshall Rosenberg, highlights this point, as well. In NVC, emotions point to universal human needs.[71] Frustration might indicate a need for autonomy. Sadness might reflect a longing for connection. Anger might show us where we feel violated or unseen. The more we understand this, and learn to connect the dots between what we feel and what we need, the more wisdom is revealed. This means identifying unmet needs and then being able to take action based on that, as opposed to attributing blame or making demands.

Acceptance and Commitment Therapy (ACT) also views emotions as doorways. In ACT, emotions act as signposts for deeply held values.[72] Painful emotions often arise when something we care about is being threatened. Feeling grief after a friendship fades might reveal that connection and loyalty are core values. Recognizing this connection—between emotions and our values—helps us take action that's better aligned with what we care about, rather than getting stuck in reactivity or avoidance.

Realistically, we can't take action—in a traditional sense—on every single issue out there. There just aren't enough hours in the day, nor would it be appropriate. We're not all positioned to work directly on many things— think of food distribution in war zones or rescue missions in forest fires. But what we can do through collective healing is uncover deeply held values about life and our roles in it. We can use these insights to live a more values-centered life.

On a spiritual level, emotions can also reveal something larger than the immediate situation. What bigger-picture wisdom emerges when we fully move through an emotion? Has anger sharpened our clarity about what must be defended? Has grief softened something inside us, offering a new perspective? In moments of stillness—when we have sat with an emotion, without bypassing or rushing it—what comes through? Maybe it arrives as an image, a somatic knowing, or a quiet, intuitive shift. Maybe it is simply a felt truth that takes root inside us.

Even in the face of existential questions—the riddles without clear answers, the ones we are being asked to live in our complex world these days— moving through emotions helps us address the unknown with more grace.

Poet Rainer Maria Rilke offers wisdom for this:

"Be patient toward all that is unsolved in your heart and try to love the questions themselves... Do not now seek the answers, which cannot be

given you because you would not be able to live them. And the point is, to live everything. Live the questions now. Perhaps you will then gradually, without noticing it, live along some distant day into the answer." [73]

Trust what comes through

"I wanted you to tell me what to do, but I found something much deeper." – Ruby, artist

I knew exactly what she meant. As Ruby left the final Circle in my series on racial justice, her words came out almost like an exhale.

In her comment, I heard so much: anxiety about what to do, fear of doing it wrong (*whatever "it" is*), the intensity of a topic like racism, and the dynamic that someone outside of her could give her all the answers.

Maybe you can relate to that? I find that a lot of people I know can. The political climate in our country—exasperated by the digital nature of things—creates such an impulse to be up in each other's faces. "*The world is on fire!*" is the sentiment. "*If you're not doing X, Y, and Z then YOU'RE part of the problem!*"

The urgency and perceived severity (*rightly or wrongly*) of these issues makes them hot to hold. As advocates of social change, there's a real pressure to persuade others by being loud and bold. How else do we get our points across? How else will people know "the truth?!"

That exhale in Ruby's words point to something else, something that's needed in the face of uncertainty and complexity. It's wisdom.

The type of wisdom I'm talking about, though, isn't some sort of singular truth or pre-determined lesson. In Circle, we don't dictate what someone should walk away with or expect all of us to arrive at the same conclusions. Instead, we trust that we each receive what we need to receive from the process.

Trust like this is the key to allowing things to emerge, instead of forcing things into existence. It is an antidote to the cultural impulse to push, force, and control, especially as it relates to the world. Yes, it is necessary at times to use willpower to manifest things or get them done. However, when it comes to wisdom, we can't manufacture or impose it on others. Instead, it emerges when the right conditions are in place.

This is what healing does—it doesn't give us wisdom; it creates the right conditions for wisdom to emerge. Therefore, a principle of practice is to set up those conditions and trust what comes through.

It's quite a radical notion, if you think about it. This idea that we all have what we need. It means that what arises—within us and between us—has a purpose, even if we don't understand it in the moment. It pushes us to believe in the divine intelligence of each other's journeys, and how that is inherently part of the collective's. By each of us being authentically ourselves, and by bringing our stories and experiences forward, we'll each receive what we need to receive for our unique role in the world.

People don't like being told what to do. It's a fault within the world—thinking that if we pressure and shame people into doing new things, it will have lasting effects. Part of this time of liberation and consciousness shifts is greater freedom to choose. What we believe, who we want to be, and how we show up. We need to support each other to arrive at our own conclusions. Put down the arrogance that believes we know what's best for one another.

Designed for shared wisdom

None of us has all the answers, but all of us have wisdom to offer.

This creed has been at the heart of collective healing for me since day one. It speaks to the need—and opportunity—to co-create wisdom together about what's going on: to trust that the nature of the things we're grappling with requires this of us.

Are you familiar with the ancient Indian myth about the blind men coming across an elephant for the first time? Each one is at a different part of the elephant, describing what they feel. The man at the trunk says, *"It's long and snake-like, like a hose!"* The man at the foot says, *"No, no it's dense and round, more like a tree stump!"* The man at the tail says, *"You're both wrong. It's thin and bristly like a paint brush!"*

This is us as a collective right now. Grappling in the dark, trying to make sense of the behemoth we can feel in front of us. Collective healing as a practice sees this as an opportunity, which is why the next principle is about shared wisdom.

Circle space is a place that allows diverse voices to express themselves and teach each other. Like the blind men and the elephant, it allows the different parts that we each sense to be shared so we get a little closer to the whole.

In Circle, we practice sitting on equal footing with each other. We step into the space with a stance of humility, knowing that, although we have much to offer, we are not the teacher. Instead, our current moment is the teacher. Now we get to weave together the various puzzle pieces we each have in order to get a little closer to something that resembles wholeness. Perhaps we hear this lesson in our own story, perhaps we hear it in another's, or perhaps we hear it in the silence in between.

As Otto Scharmer said:

> *"Our highest teacher within this work isn't an individual or a Guru. Our highest teacher is the reality of our times—the social, ecological, economic, and energetic systems we live in and the disruptions we're experiencing. Our ability to be aware of and present with these changes, and sense into the emerging future that's taking form."*[74]

In practice, this looks like grounding our stories in our own personal lived experiences and being mindful to not prescribe or go into teacher mode. We refrain from cross-talk, and instead are encouraged to be inspired by what each other says, but to ground our responses in our own lived experiences. The desire to teach one another is admirable but it also carries assumptions, compromises the safety of the group, and shifts the power dynamics. It puts you above the other person. Moreover, it gives something that the other person didn't ask for. Trust that everyone has what they need, and that, if they don't, they'll ask for it. Instead, let's say someone shares something and your impulse is to recommend an article. Instead of saying, *"Hey! Check out this article..."* Make your experience with the article the center of your share. Why does that article come to mind for you? What did it offer you and why?

The structure of the Circle and the way it's facilitated foster co-creation. The design of the space shifts power away from being hierarchical towards being horizontal. It redistributes the power to be equally shared by all, instead of one leader or person holding it. Instead, we all contribute.

A generative, well-held community container has a nice balance of structure and flexibility. Group settings can sometimes suffer from one person (*often the teacher, leader, or facilitator*) taking up a lot of space; being the person who is seen to have all of the answers, and is thus deferred to for their wisdom. On the flip side, they can also suffer from a lack of well-designed structure: too much openness, if you will. No one knows what their role is or who's in charge or what the norms of engagement are. Is it okay for me to speak? What will happen if I do?

Neither of these scenarios support people to feel safe or empowered to co-create the space. A guiding approach is to find a balance between having enough structure that people don't have to worry about what's coming next—they can sink into their experience and go for a ride, knowing they're being taken care of—with the active and implicit honoring of everyone's wisdom as worthwhile.

Learn through shapeshifting

"In these Circles, people's stories provide architecture for me to step into and ground new learnings in." – Andy, circular economy entrepreneur

Resonance practice offers Circle space so much. In addition to all the other things I've shared, another advantage is that it helps listeners cultivate the capacity for embodied empathy. This is the kind that allows them to step into the story someone else is telling, try it on for size, and walk away with any new learnings or insights that are well-suited to them.

By slowing down and attuning to the subtle energy of what is being shared, we allow ourselves to be empathetic in a way that is embodied, not purely cognitive. We learn through shapeshifting. We shift our shape to match that of another. We step into their life experiences and take away deep learnings beyond the mind.

Did you know that there are two different types of empathy? Cognitive empathy and affective empathy. Each one activates different parts of our brains.

Cognitive empathy is the type in which a person can take on another person's perspective at a mental level. They can cognitively understand someone else's position, circumstances, or line of thinking. They can put themselves "in their shoes," if you will.

Affective empathy, on the other hand, is the type of empathy in which a person seems to directly share an emotional or affective state with someone else. There is the probability that Person A's mirror neurons fire when they see Person B's emotional experience or hear their story.[75] The experience of sensory information that comes with this type of empathy is not cognitive but affective—meaning emotional—and somatic. They don't just put themselves in another person's shoes; they actually walk around in them.

Through resonance practice, we empathically step into each other's stories and an embodied learning takes place. When you listen to someone's story with your whole body, you are transported into their world, in real time. You can sense the energetic frequency of the person's story, and the wisdom held in it. And because you're doing so with your somatic and emotional bodies, you have an opportunity to take information home which is connected to deeper layers of your being.

When it comes to collective healing and being a conduit for our changing times, this type of embodied learning gives us an opportunity to receive things that perhaps our body is able to know, but our mind is not ready to yet. Perhaps there is a bone-level knowing we have about the state of the world and where we are going that our minds cannot compute. Or guidance coming through from our ancestors that does not translate clearly into our current cultural understanding of things. Perhaps the language we have for a topic or issue is not sufficient. It is keeping us stuck. Therefore, activating our ability to sense and know in different ways gives us access to something that we would have missed otherwise.

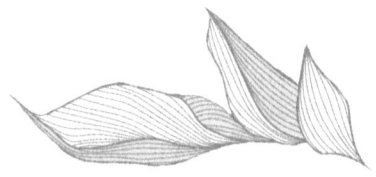

Chapter 9

BRING IT INTO YOUR LIFE

GUIDING PRINCIPLES:

Bring it into your life. Put those insights into practice by integrating them into your life.

> » First, integrate
> » Weave it into your life
> » Take an inside-out approach

Create Space   Process   Unearth Wisdom   **Bring it into your life**   Be Supported

Now that you've unearthed wisdom, the next task is to bring those insights into your life.

Sure, yeah! Let's do it. That might be your internal response. But let's be real—putting our insights into practice is hard. It's hard to live in a world that doesn't reflect our values, or to be constantly navigating a moral universe that's in flux.

Maybe through this collective healing practice you realized how important it is to actually talk with your pretty (*okay, very*) transphobic cousin instead of rolling your eyes and brushing him off—or worse, screaming at him and then not talking for two years. Something inside you is pushing you to do it, and you were able to create space for that something, and now understand it better.

It's now time to put those realizations—and the new resources you have within yourself—into play. To take that risk, put yourself out there, and try something new the next time he makes that comment.

This is what we'll unpack in this section: how to take what you unearthed and bring it into your life. We'll see how to do so in a way that is a practice in and of itself, instead of something you always need to get right. We'll look at principles of practices that can help us to do this important stage, so we can be of service and lovingly shift culture through the way we live our lives.

When you go to do something new or hard, what is your process like? Especially after a big ah-hah moment or realization, what types of things support you to harness that energy and put it into action? If you work with others, what things help them integrate insights into their life in real, meaningful ways?

First, integrate

Within the context of collective healing, an important step needs to happen between receiving guidance and putting it into practice. It's an opportunity to metaprocess what you just discovered and take time to let it land in your body.

Ah-hah moments—like the ones that can emerge during the *Unearth Wisdom* portion of collective healing—can be thrilling. A light bulb goes on. A new lens on life takes shape. It can be ecstatic, really. There's often a surge of energy that comes with seeing something clearly for the first time. By the end of a storytelling round, you might be walking on cloud nine.

At the same time, emotional release can leave us feeling tender or raw. Sharing a part of your heart for the first time, or letting a tiny crackle in your voice finally come through, can stretch us in ways that need care before we re-enter the world. That tenderness is part of the healing—but it also means we need space to metabolize the experience.

This is why having time to integrate what just happened before returning to everyday life is key. Without that pause, the energy can dissipate quickly. Insights can slip away. Emotional openings can leave us ungrounded. A big moment of transformation, if not supported properly, can fade or even destabilize.

So how do we help people—and ourselves—carry the energy and insights with us when we leave the Circle? Is it enough to simply walk away, hoping to stay in that frequency? Or is there another step that can help us hold onto what just emerged more fully?

The healing-centered sciences give us the term *metaprocess*—a moment to reflect on what it was like to have the experience you just had. [76] It often comes at the end of therapy or any transformational encounter, and it's essentially a way to process what just happened—to process the processing, if you will. What was it like to have that insight? How did it feel to experience that release? What has changed, even subtly, since the beginning of the session?

Metaprocessing invites us to zoom out from the emotional content or insight we were knee-deep in, and gently reflect on our experience to integrate it. It's not about analyzing or breaking it apart—it's about noticing, letting it land, and giving your system time to catch up with what just moved through it.

In Circle, this often takes the form of a closing meditation, prayer, or exercise. I like to offer a brief practice that invites people to connect with that which is greater than them, whatever that might mean—whether that's Planet Earth, the Universe, the system, or the human family. From a healing perspective, it serves as a wind-down: an invitation to notice what you're carrying now compared to when we began, how your body feels, and what you're taking with you. From a spiritual perspective, it becomes an offering—an opportunity to offer up the energy that was conjured together to something greater than ourselves, and to return some of that energy to the greater whole.

We don't just do this work for ourselves. Part of social change and collective liberation is understanding ourselves as part of something larger. That means tending to the transitions between the inner and the outer—between insight and action, and between self and world.

If we don't give ourselves time to integrate, we risk bypassing the very wisdom we uncovered. We risk moving too quickly, staying in the high, or burning out on the rawness. Metaprocessing helps us slow down, create meaning, and prepare to carry what we've discovered forward—so that healing can ripple outward with integrity.

Solo Practice

Metaprocessing on your own can look like taking a few minutes at the end of journaling (*or any other process you're doing to support yourself*) to zoom out and notice what it was like to have had the experience you just had. Maybe you journal more, metaprocessing your experience that way. Or maybe you call up a friend and talk about it with them.

Weave it into your life

So now what?

You've processed. You've unearthed wisdom. You've taken the time to integrate what came through. Now comes the part where you weave it into your life.

The end goal of collective healing work isn't just to feel better in private (*although, that's nice*). It's about taking what we discover when we create space for our inner worlds and bring those insights into our lives to be of service to the outer world.

This has benefits for us and for the collective. When we're better able to move about the world from a place of aligned action and with a clearer moral conscience, this helps our vitality and sense of self. We're more whole, not having to spend so much energy battling the parts of ourselves that are guilt-ridden, confused, or slogged down by _____ (*modernity, the rat race, systems of oppression… you fill in the blank*).

It also helps the collective. This process helps us step more fully into the unique role we're meant to play during this time—in our projects, activism, work life, and relationships. We walk away better resourced for the against-the-grain work that is change-making.

As I mentioned in the opening invitation of this book, a changemaker is anyone who is consciously aware that the way they live their life affects the world around them, and therefore chooses to do so in intentional ways. Vera Luísa Franco, Possibility Management trainer and coach, uses the term "cultural edge worker"[77] to describe this: someone who's shaping the evolving edge of culture through the way they live their life.

This cultural edge work requires us to experiment. To use our lives as a living laboratory, if you will, where we test and prototype new ways of being or types of action to see how it lands, how it feels, and how it goes. In this way, we're both pioneers and guinea pigs. Pioneers in that we're charting a new path at the edge of the cultural frontier. And guinea pigs in that we use our lives as a sandbox to experiment and play, knowing it'll include slip-ups and back-slides. The castles we built that are a perfect fit for today may wash away with the rain by tomorrow. So we need to be adaptable and flexible in our pursuit of finding the right toys and tools to bring along for the long haul.

As I touched upon in the Unearth Wisdom section, when we get clearer on what our values are—the ones embedded in the emotions we feel—we are better able to move about the world from a place of aligned action. We can more skillfully meet our own needs as they relate to the world, which comes from living our values.

By coming into greater contact with our values—getting clearer about what they are—we can learn to live them in strong, steady ways that have ripple effects. There's a form of leadership within this, a subtle one. Our presence becomes of service through the way we live.

So where do you begin? Bringing this work to life looks different for everyone. Some of us need to move first and reflect later. Others need to get clear inside before stepping out. Most of us bounce between inner and outer work, discovering what's needed as we go. The prompts below offer different entry points—jump in wherever it feels right for you.

For the outward movers (those ready to experiment in the world)
- » What's one small experiment I can try this week?
- » What's already in motion around me I could join—groups, projects, or efforts?
- » What roles do I already play that could become spaces for practice?
- » What types of action best suit who I am? (writing, organizing, caring, creating?)

For the inner reorganizers (those needing to shift internal patterns first)
- » What old ways of helping or being "productive" am I ready to let go of?
- » What keeps calling to me that I've been putting off?
- » In what ways am I already living my values that I haven't been giving myself credit for?
- » What vision or feeling of aliveness can guide my choices? How can I stay connected to that?
- » What boundaries or non-negotiables are my hard nos?

For the bridge builders (those working with relationships and community)
- » Who are my people—who else is living similar values, even if differently?
- » What relationships could become spaces for mutual exploration?
- » Where do I already have influence or access?
- » What conversations have I been avoiding that want to happen?
- » How can I stay connected to my why when I'm the only one who sees things this way?

For the sustainers (those focused on making it a practice)
- » What rhythm of activity actually works with my real life?
- » What's my game plan for when I inevitably stumble?
- » What tells me if this is life-giving versus performative versus burdensome?
- » What nourishes me enough to keep showing up?

Take an inside-out approach

Culture change is a big conversation within the sustainable development and social impact space. How do we change society's culture to be more just, inclusive, healthy, regenerative, and peaceful? For us as changemakers, it's a big driver for why we want to be of service.

At the heart of questions about culture change are the people it comprises—the behaviors and attitudes that the people who are part of that culture hold. Therefore, policy and interventions that have the goal of culture change are often designed to target people through behavioral change. How do we shift people's behaviors when it comes to things like food waste, racial prejudice, conspicuous consumption, or the sexualization of women? Think Diversity, Equity, and Inclusion (DEI) trainings in corporations, or handwashing campaigns in rural India.

These initiatives rely on an outside-in approach to culture change. Meaning, they deliver skills or provide education to a group of people to try to shift behavior. They operate on the assumption that we can shift the way people act, behave, or think by giving them skills or ideas they don't already have.

This makes sense, right? If a group of people needs skills to change, receiving those skills is helpful. An outside-in approach like this is necessary and effective sometimes.

There are ways, though, that it's not always effective. In some cases, it's incomplete. Think back to the DEI trainings I referenced. They're a great way to learn certain terminology, ideas, and skills, such as the idea of equity versus equality, or what a microaggression is. However, to shift something like an implicit bias or prejudiced view, people need an opportunity to unpack their inner worlds and understand themselves in a supportive and psychologically safe environment.

This is what collective healing provides.

So often, those of us who strive to be socially conscious, good people can find ourselves feeling defeated and at a loss when it comes to shifting certain behaviors we want to change. Maybe it's a shopping habit. Or a propensity towards porn. Maybe you had a bad encounter with someone who looks a certain way and now notice a subconscious guardedness in yourself when you encounter others who remind you of them.

Shifting things like this aren't just a matter of willpower or shaming the change into existence. Sure, bullying ourselves (*or others for that matter*) can give us some short-term wins. But ultimately, true transformation requires a different approach, one that moves from the inside-out. Which is why it's a principle within this collective healing practice.

When it comes to taking action in the world, it's important to keep the value of an inside-out approach in mind as you go. When the going gets tough, and we fail to adopt the habits we want to adopt or embody the leadership approaches we are striving for, seeing the bigger picture of how transformation comes about is key.

The healing-centered sciences teach us that pro-social qualities—like compassion, open-mindedness, and humility—aren't something that can be taught by someone outside of us; instead, they are unlocked from within us through authentic healing.[78] Believe it or not, these pro-social qualities are natural and inherent to all of us. We just need the right support and conditions to cultivate them and help them come through.

In a world that often relies too much on outside-in approaches, collective healing sees culture change as something that requires an inside-out approach to behavioral change and any sort of sustained action.

Chapter 10

BE SUPPORTED

GUIDING PRINCIPLES:

Be supported. In an ongoing fashion through community and more.

- » In this, together
- » Change is ongoing, so is this practice
- » Embedded in something greater

Create
Space

Process

Unearth
Wisdom

Bring it into
your life

Be
Supported

So here we are, putting our values to work, experimenting as we go, and doing the best we can to show up authentically in this changing world.

This is no small task. Using your life to be a conduit for change means going against the grain in many cases. Choosing to be proactive these days, and not let the challenges of our time swallow you up, takes effort! The volatile nature of things also means this work is a moving target, requiring us to stay adaptable as changes come.

Many of us feel isolated and overwhelmed, especially if we're lone wolves in our families trying to live differently, or on an island in our companies embodying values others don't share. We need support, which is why the final pillar in our collective healing practice is to be supported.

If you're not tired of me saying this by now, this collective healing practice isn't about finding a single "fix" to a given problem or figuring out how not to be mad about what's going on. Instead, it's about building an ongoing relationship with ourselves and the world—one that better equips us to show up and respond.

Being supported helps us do so. It turns all of this into a practice instead of a one-and-done task. It helps us stay in it for the long haul and find ways to make sure we're spiritually and morally fed along the way. It reminds us that while we might be swimming upstream, we're part of something larger—a constellation of people who are also committed to this work, even if it looks different from ours.

What comes to mind for you when you think about being supported? Especially within the context of collective healing. What types of support have been most nourishing or generative for you? What haven't? What type of support do you want to see more of in the world?

In this, together

Finding people you can go along for the ride with is so important. It's important in life in general, and especially so when it comes to being in relationship with the world. We need to feel seen and heard by others who get what we're doing and celebrate our wins. We need people who nudge us when we get complacent or slip into perfectionism; people who can help us be the versions of ourselves we want to be.

The weight of the world is heavy; too heavy to carry on our own. Being with resonant others helps normalize this reality and distribute the load, which makes it more bearable. Support like this helps us when we run into inevitable burnout, uncertainty, and stuckness.

At a time when our social order and the moral fabric that holds it together are in a process of change, we need to find our people to give birth to what's meant to come next. As Dr. Anita Brock, professor at Union Theological Seminary, says, "*We didn't become moral beings on our own, so we can't reconstruct our moral universe on our own.*"[79] We need to come together in a community to co-create new threads of insight and wisdom that can be used to rethread our shared fabric. We can create microcosms of the world we want to see more of.

Finding your people is a practice of discernment, as well. The good thing about this age of social consciousness is that there are many people and communities out there who are striving to make the world a better place. Interestingly, though, this makes finding the people who are going about change-making in a similar way to you even more important. Not everyone is wired to march in the streets, speak on stages, or work inside institutions—and that's a good thing. There are many different ways to contribute, and your people are often those who affirm your way of doing things: the ones who help you stay connected to your values, who don't pressure you to perform, but instead help you live what matters most.

Here are ways to think about finding your people:

> » You feel comfortable around them and know they'll hold you
> accountable to staying true to yourself. They'll call you on your
> BS while also making space for your whole messy evolution.
> There's space for all of your parts, including the ways parts of
> you change and evolve over time.

» Look for spiritual communities, personal development groups, or wellness spaces that don't pretend the world isn't on fire. These groups often work at the intersection of inner and outer change, or have pockets of their community that do so.

» One way to find your people is to ask: "Who's going about this stuff in a way that resonates with me?"

» Find those who care about process just as much as outcomes. People who understand that how we go about change matters just as much as what we're trying to change.

» The good thing about everyday changemakers is that… we're everywhere! So look outside of formal activist or organizing spaces to parenting circles, book clubs, staff meetings, yoga studios. Keep an open mind about where you might find people to connect with on this.

Part of discernment is naming your non-negotiables—the behaviors or dynamics you're unwilling to compromise on in yourself or others. In the same way that we clarify what brings us to life, it's just as important to get honest about what drains us, distorts us, or pulls us off course. You deserve to be in spaces where your inner wisdom is met with respect, not confusion or contempt. Boundaries are not about exclusion or control—they're about protection and care, so you can maintain integrity and keep showing up in ways that feel true.

Change is ongoing, so is this practice

When I was younger, I used to believe that if I could just heal all my wounds, I'd reach some kind of state of completion—maybe enlightenment. I extended that idea to society too: "*If only everyone healed their trauma, then the world would* ____ [fill in the blank]."

There was a final destination in my mind that came with this notion of healing. That healing will get us somewhere, and that somewhere looked a specific way—more harmonious, green, multicultural, regenerative, and free.

While that vision of the future is still with me, I've come to realize that that's not how healing works—or social change, for that matter. Healing won't deliver us somewhere specific. It doesn't promise a certain outcome or set of policy solutions. Instead, it gives us a tool to work with uncertainty.

Healing trauma won't cure the world, resolve every crisis, or eliminate pain. Instead, it offers us something more real—a way to be in relationship with the world as it changes and to work with the pain and possibility of this moment… and the next moment, and the next. Because while healing may not permanently transmute darkness into light and keep it that way forever, it *does* help us stay with the mess and roll with the punches—the ones that are here and that have yet to come.

In a world changing as quickly as ours, actions and policies we feel confident about today can become outdated within months. The right move today may be the wrong one tomorrow. There are no definitive answers out there about the problems we face. So we need tools that help us stay present, discerning, and flexible—able to ebb and flow with the ongoing sea of change.

This is why we have to treat this change-making work as a practice, not a destination, and collective healing supports us to do that. It creates the space we need to listen to the emotional intelligence in this moment and respond from there. It is an ongoing process that matches the dynamic nature of the times. Instead of delivering us somewhere specific, it'll support whatever things need to develop for what's in front of us.

When we approach change-making in this way, we build our capacity for uncertainty. We stop bracing against the unknown and begin relating to it. We become more attuned to what wants to emerge, and more available to what's needed next.

Maybe most importantly, we support ourselves to keep going. Not because we know exactly where we're going—but because we have tools to help as we go.

Embedded in something greater

At the close of every Circle, we take time to turn our attention outward. We do so to connect with that which is greater than ourselves and offer the energy we created to it. I often guide a meditation that helps us do so— to tune into the Earth, Universe, ancestors, the collective field—whatever feels meaningful to each person. It's an opportunity to give back what we received, and a chance to remember that what just moved through us didn't begin or end here—it's part of something bigger.

As one Circle participant, Michael, once said, "*It's like there's some kind of tending to our collective body that we do here. So that we can all—in our own way as individuals, but also as a collective—go back out and engage with the world in all these different ways.*"

Feeling yourself embedded within something greater than yourself is one of the most life-giving forms of support that this collective healing practice offers. Whether that something bigger is a social movement, a family lineage, the unfolding of human history, the spirit of your ancestors, or a higher moral or spiritual purpose, there's power in remembering you're not doing this alone. You're part of a living, breathing whole.

Part of the work of collective healing is learning how to feel that, and to let yourself be nourished by it. It's an opportunity to practice change-making not just as a personal conviction, but as a contribution to something greater that's unfolding.

It helps make the work sustainable. It connects you to a deeper source of energy. It grounds you in a "why" at the heart of your work, even when it's hard. This guiding principle is about identifying what that source connection looks like for you, and creating ways to connect with it.

Embedding what you're doing into something greater than yourself reminds you that you're not just pushing against something—you're participating in something. And that something is beautiful. It's messy, yes. It's in flux. But it's also sacred, and you are part of it.

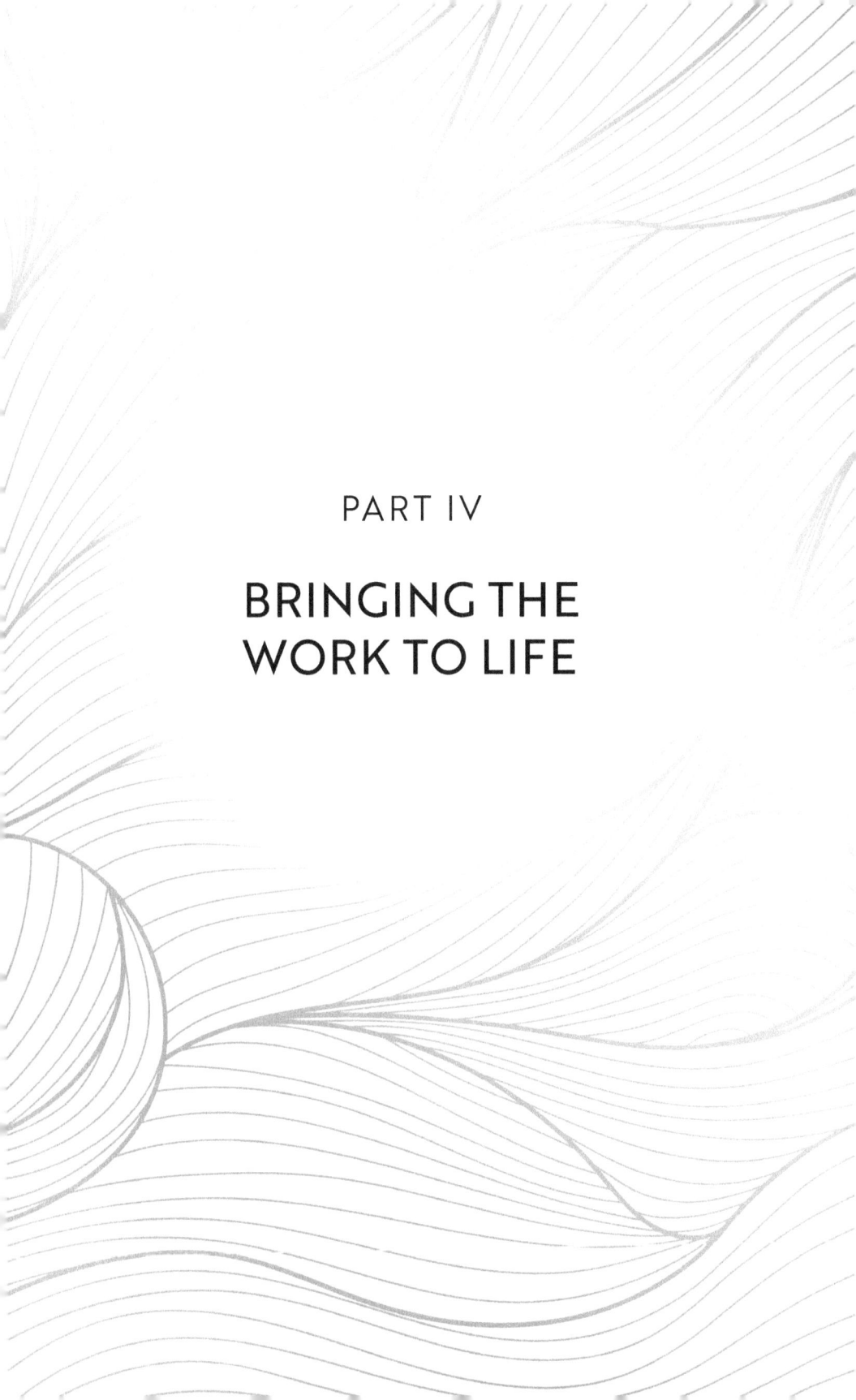

PART IV

BRINGING THE
WORK TO LIFE

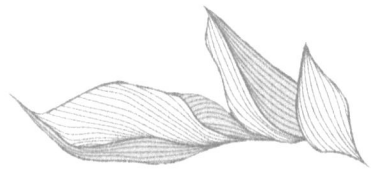

Chapter 11

WORKING WITH
COLLECTIVE WOUNDS

I n the last chapter, we explored the practice of collective healing—how
to work with what we feel about the world for our own heart's and the
collective's well-being.

We learned ways we can better hold all that we feel. Now, in this chapter, I
want to invite us to better understand exactly *what* it is that we're holding. If the
previous chapter offered practices for working with the world's pain, this one
helps us understand what that pain is made of—specifically, collective wounds.

In the pages ahead, we'll look at what collective wounds are and how they
show up in us. This awareness helps us understand ourselves better—why
certain topics speak to us more than others, and why we may react the way
we do. It also helps us understand others—letting us listen below the surface of their stories and meet them there, which feels especially important
in these fraught political times.

My hope is that you'll walk away with frameworks that help you think
about collective wounds and identify which parts of your experience may
be tied to them. Awareness like this is the first step in healing. While I won't
go into healing techniques in depth here, this awareness lays the foundation for deeper work like that to unfold.

You're invited to bring everything we just explored into this next chapter. The practice of collective healing is still with us. We're just orienting our awareness toward a specific, and often unseen dimension of what many of us are feeling.

What I will share here is an exploration more than a scientific method. It's a part of the experience of being in relationship with the world that we don't have language for, and which often goes unseen as a result. My goal with this chapter is to attempt to offer up language and framing to this aspect of things, in the hope that it gets us a bit closer to a shared understanding of what collective wounds are and how they manifest.

What are collective wounds?

As the world becomes more complicated and I, as a 21st century human, have a greater awareness of it all, there's a growing need for me to figure out how to be in relationship with all of the emotional energy that comes with it. Emotional energy that is my own, for sure. That is my own stress and distress about the state of things—my own sadness and fatigue. But then also emotional energy that is beyond me. That isn't limited to my personal edges. That is instead part of the collective body that I am a part of: the emotional energy of society's collective wounds.

Collective wounds come in all shapes and sizes. Some of them are specifically experienced by certain communities and family lineages, due to histories of conflict, oppression, or tragedy. Others are shared across a whole country, such as experiences of war or pandemics. Then there are others felt by identity groups that span different areas, such as shared experiences of injustice or alienation.

Collective wounds vary in their relationship with time; they can relate to historical and intergenerational trauma tied to the past, or anxiety and uncertainty about the future. As individuals, we each have our own unique set of experiences with different types of collective wounds based on our personal history, personality, orientation, and more.

Wounds held by a collective body

Any time a group of people have a shared experience of pain, distress, harm, chaos, injustice, or violence, there is the potential for a collectively-held emotional wound to form. It can be thought of as imprinted emotional energy that a collective body of people carries. Individual members of the group feel it in different ways and have varying levels of sensitivity to it.

It also exists beyond individual members, similar to Durkheim's concept of the collective consciousness. (*I hope Durkheim won't roll over in his grave due to me invoking this*). If you recall, Durkheim saw the collective consciousness as something that is "distinctly separate from us as individuals, and is instead an extension of the larger web of society."[80] I believe this is the same for our collective emotional body.

An example of a collective wound that comes to mind is when a school or community experiences a mass shooting. After the heinous event, some people may feel extreme anger; they may be furious at the shooter or authorities. Others may feel overwhelmingly despondent that events like this keep happening. Meanwhile, others may be in a state of shock and disbelief that it happened in *their* community.

Each individual member of the community has their own unique experience in response to what happened. Then there is also a set of emotional energy that is carried by the community or collective body itself. The pain and trauma that occurred can be felt in school assemblies, PTA meetings, and the halls of the school building. The school becomes known for this heinous atrocity and its name is associated with the shooting both locally and nationally. The event changes the structural makeup of the school itself, both in terms of new policies and the safety measures put in place. Newly installed metal detectors at the school entrance serve as a daily reminder of the incident. The sound of a loud bang or the alarm going off triggers a collective gasp and hypervigilance among students and teachers.

Even if one community member does the tremendous work to process and heal their experience—let's say in therapy—they return to a community still carrying that wound. Personal healing doesn't shield you from collective pain—you still have to navigate relationships, spaces, and dynamics shaped by the unprocessed grief around you. Which is why community-based healing matters so much.

The (big picture) opportunity inside collective wounds

Recognizing collective wounds isn't just an intellectual exercise; it has practical implications for us and society. A core idea behind this chapter—and this whole book—is that collectively-held wounds within society affect the way it operates. When crises erupt or the need for change arises, collective wounds affect the way the system and the people in it respond.

The good news? In this era of heightened self-awareness as a system, collective wounds are in our faces in new ways these days. Since they're so front and center, it gives us a powerful opening to work with them constructively, and hopefully aid in society's transformation.

What we're exploring here is a bridge between what we know about personal healing and what might be possible at the collective level. If we can work with the collective wounds that society carries more constructively —really see them, feel them, and tend to them—we may be able to create the conditions for change that runs deeper than policy or reform. We can get at some of the emotional roots of old, outdated cultural patterns like exploitation and disconnection, helping them heal and transform into new potential—skills, qualities, and ways of being—for society.

Wounds versus emotions

Throughout this chapter, I talk about collective wounds and emotions. Before we move forward, I want to briefly clarify the difference between the two.

A wound refers to a rupture or imbalance within a system—something that happened (or didn't happen) that left a lasting mark on someone or a collective body. They are often tied to unmet human needs (like safety, dignity, or belonging) that haven't been addressed or healed.

An emotion is the way our system—individually or collectively—communicates the fact that the wound is there. It is sensory information that tells us something is out of balance. In this way, emotions act as messengers that signal that something is unresolved, unacknowledged, or in need. They're our nervous system's way of letting us know where to turn our attention.

As you consider the idea of collective wounds, where does your attention go? Do certain stories, places, images, or communities come to mind? If so, what do you notice about them?

Do we really feel collective wounds?

The idea that parts of our personal lived experiences are tied to the collective can be a tricky thing to wrap your head around. It can sound a bit sci-fi (*or a lot sci-fi*), and it also brings us nose-to-nose with our own philosophical understanding of what emotions are and how we, as humans, work.

Are we solely confined to the limits of our individual minds and bodies? Or do we exist in webs of relationality—emotional, social, and ancestral—that shape us?

If parts of your experience with the world's pain feel bigger than you—like they're not entirely yours—you're not imagining it. Several disciplines offer insight into how this might be possible. Here are three sources of thought that inform my understanding of collective wounds:

Parts work and the plural self

In many schools of psychotherapy, particularly Internal Family Systems and attachment-based models, the human psyche is seen as plural.[81] We are made up of many "parts"—younger selves, protector parts, and wise selves—each with their own needs and motivations. This model helps us name, care for, and integrate the complexity within us.

Carl Jung expanded this idea beyond the personal psyche, suggesting that we're also shaped by archetypal energies in the collective unconscious.[82] From this view, some of the "parts" that show up in us may not be purely personal, but instead tied to the collective. Seeing ourselves through this lens helps us recognize when a part of what we feel might be connected to a larger emotional field.

The tribal soul

In Family Constellations work[83]—a systemic healing modality—individual challenges are often traced to unresolved pain in the family or ancestral field. Daan van Kampenhout expands on this with the concept of the *tribal soul*,[84] a layer of soul shared by any collective that defines itself as distinct (e.g., nations, political groups, or cultural communities).[85]

Each tribal soul has its own emotional history. As individuals, we may feel those histories—the grief, rage, or longing—not just as personal reactions, but as echoes of the collective field we belong to. As van Kampenhout writes: *"Although it may be true that I have an individual soul, it is equally true that the tribal soul has me."*[86]

Practices like constellation work and collective healing allow us to interact with these subtle fields, making space for emotional material that doesn't belong only to us, but that we're connected to through the collective field.[87]

Empathy and relational neuroscience

As we discussed earlier, neuroscience teaches us that there's a difference between cognitive empathy and affective empathy. The latter is when we can actually feel another person's emotional state. It's a sign of our relational wiring.

Our nervous systems are socially responsive. Polyvagal Theory shows that our physiological state is shaped by the people around us, especially those in close proximity.[88] As described earlier, a mother helps regulate her infant's emotions through her own calm presence.

While these findings come from a worldview that sees us as self-contained individuals, they reveal something profound—we literally share sensory and emotional experiences through affective empathy. The fact that neuroscience confirms that two people can share an emotional state points to a biophysical indicator of our collective interdependence.

All of this lends itself to the idea that what is happening in the world affects us as individuals. We can feel collective wounds—those carried by different groups and born from different circumstances—because we're neurologically wired for this kind of attunement.

What's it like to consider that some of what you feel might not originate solely from you?

Take a breath and turn your attention inward. Name a tribal soul group that you're part of. "I am part of the [group/identity/national] tribal soul." What do you notice? What images, feelings, or memories come up as you sit with this?

How do they show up in us? Jaleel's story

Okay, so collective wounds exist—but what might that actually look like in a person? Now that we've laid the foundations of what collective wounds are, let's build out our understanding by looking at how they show up in us, beginning with my friend Jaleel.

As a heads up—this section incudes descriptions of the war in Gaza, such as deprivation and children's suffering. Please choose what is best for you and whether, right now, in this moment, you're in a place to engage with this content.

Meet Jaleel

Meet Jaleel, a dear friend of mine who I had the honor of working with throughout the development of this book. He has generously given me permission to share his collective healing process with you here.

Jaleel is 42 years old. He is a thoughtful and creative human: a software engineer by day, and a musician by night. His parents immigrated to the United States from Tunisia in the 1980s.

As an Arab-American, the Israel-Hamas war in Gaza has hit home for him in more ways than one. His process of figuring out how to be in relationship with the world's pain and, specifically, the pain of the Gazan people, and Muslims and Jews the world over, has brought up wounds related to his identity, his family lineage, his childhood, and the world at large.

Jaleel and I sat down together to hold space for everything he was feeling. This was in March of 2024, five months into the war.

With both of us together in the comfort of my home, we sat across from each other, making our bodies as comfortable as possible. What follows is the collective healing process we did together, and the specific parts of his experience that came up.

Thank you, Jaleel.

Jaleel's process

As we open the space, an image of a child in Gaza comes forward for Jaleel. The six-year old boy's body is withered — emaciated, really. His face has dirt markings on it and his eyes are sunken. There is rubble in the background.

Jaleel's own face gets heavy as this image appears. His eyes look downward and the rest of his body follows, sinking in on itself. The deep, unbearable tragedy is clearly heavy for him.

We slow down to attune ourselves to his experience. He notices not being able to stay with the image of the child very long. His mind goes elsewhere. It is too painful and overwhelming. Too much is coming up for him to be able to stay with it.

We take our time allowing things to be slow, moving at the pace of his slowest, most tender part, being mindful not to go too quickly, and push him outside of his window of tolerance. We make sure he doesn't become dysregulated to the point of his system collapsing. Allowing his system— his mind, body, and spirit—to dictate where he wants us to go.

He notices he went to a place within himself where the memory of a podcast episode lives. He listened to it yesterday in the car. It was a left-right-and-center type of show, showcasing views from across the political spectrum.

The words of Sarah Isgur, the political pundit on the right, ripple through him as she advocates for Israel to take all military actions necessary. "We need to go in there and wipe them out." *Wipe them out.*

Anguish and frustration arise in him. Her impassioned comments reflected no sympathy for the scale of Palestinian death and suffering. No concern for the war crimes. As if awareness of these things was blocked from her mind.

Jaleel zooms out for a moment to acknowledge that he can see why she, as someone of Jewish descent, would feel the way she feels. Then he is quickly pulled back into his own feelings of disorientation and frustration as he asks himself, *"Like, what do I even do or say to that person? How can I even talk and have a conversation with someone who is so closed off from what I see? From what I know to be true."*

After a few moments of breathing, keeping his feet on the floor, and allowing the waves of feelings and energy and images and memory sensations to move through him, I ask him, *"What do you notice?"*

He says his sister Amina comes to mind; how she can't watch the news either. She stopped some time ago because it's just too much. His co-worker Yehuda comes to mind, who is one of his more devout Jewish colleagues. He wonders how he's doing, what his experience is like, how he's holding up.

Then he finds himself feeling small and alone. Powerless, really. *"There's no one here for me,"* he hears a younger part of him say. He senses into how old this part of him is, and gets back a felt sense response of probably five or six years old. His younger self sits cross-legged alone in front of the TV, wondering when his parents will be home.

Sorting through different wounds

We allow the natural rhythm of this last wave of sensory information to subside. I can see him coming back into the room we are both in. His internal gaze moves outside of himself, back towards me and the space in between us. After several moments of generous silence, I ask him for permission to name some of the collective wounds I saw. He says yes, and we do so collaboratively.

We begin with the deep, tragic, unbearable pain of the emaciated child. Pain that is his own devastated and horrified experience with the death and suffering of children, but that is also more than that. The emotional energy that came up for him during that part of the process was much bigger than just his own. We identified this part as being a bundle of collective wounds related to war, religious conflict, children and vulnerable peoples, genocide, and more. Fear about how it'll all turn out, where things will go. The multitudes within what he felt are what made it so difficult to bear.

The memory of the right-leaning political pundit's comments brought him to an interpersonal wound that stretches across issues. There is pain and confusion about how to have conversations across political lines these days. The widely differing values that exist, especially around intense and heated topics. This wound reflected feelings of disconnection, hopelessness, and exasperation. There is a woundedness in our inability to communicate with each other, to see each other, and to hear each other that came through.

Thinking about his sister and his colleague was the way his own identity-based wounds related to being a Muslim American spoke. Our minds and bodies will often communicate to us indirectly through symbolism. His mind did this by reminding him of others who also have distinct identities tied to and affected by the war. The layer related to his identity as a Muslim American is his own pain, and also a product of the larger sociopolitical fabric that his identity has developed within. Feelings of marginalization, cultural erasure, of not being seen and understood, and of being hidden came up.

Then there was a layer of his experience tied to his own personal wounds from childhood, specifically a wound of neglect. Where were the adults who were meant to protect him? Where are the metaphorical adults who are meant to protect the innocent lives of Gazan children?

The collective healing process Jaleel and I moved through together offered us an opportunity to create space for what he was feeling, and parse out different dimensions of his experience. Each one of these wounds, and the array of emotional energy that comes with them, is different and therefore in need of different things. Jaleel said it felt like each one lived somewhere a little different within him. The way the wound showed up and felt in his body was different for each one. Some lived deep in his bones, others were undulating between himself and the social fabric he is part of, and others were in an inner child part. And then there were others that were much more expansive and beyond him.

Emotions like to be named. Therefore, it was helpful to Jaleel to begin to delineate between different dimensions of his experience, so he could give each wound the support it needs. He said it was as if we had created a map of his internal world together—one he could take forward with him and reference in future.

Letting the wounds speak

As we sat together, and allowed that map to settle between us, reflections and insights about the different wounds naturally emerged. Jaleel saw how the interpersonal wound of communicating across ideological lines felt afraid, pissed off, frustrated, and shut down. It asked, "*What's the point in trying? It's not safe or productive to do so. Why bother?*" Defeat and hopelessness washed over him.

That's when Jaleel's identity-based wound related to being a Muslim American piped up from the back: "*I need you to speak up for me!*" This showed him how voiceless and terribly misunderstood this part of him feels. Jaleel turned to this part and thanked him for his courage to speak up like this. Grief washed over him. He felt such loss from this part: an excruciating aloneness and agony that comes from not being seen by others, and from not allowing himself to be seen. Tears trickled down his face as he created warm, tender space for all of it. He was letting this part know that he sees him and is committed to taking steps to better bring him into the light and heal shame and confusion.

Jaleel saw how the identity-based wound and interpersonal wound fed into each other, and that taking steps to care for one directly impacted the other. He brainstormed ways—even small ways—he could better connect with his Muslim heritage and reclaim parts of his family's history in a way that feels authentic to him.

We continued to sit together—face-to-face, our bodies across from each other—as the waves of insight and emotion slowly quieted, coming to a close. We took a deep breath together, placing our hands over our hearts. I asked him what it was like to have done this together, what he noticed as we come to a close. He said he felt more spaciousness in his body, as if some things moved that were previously stuck. He found himself feeling a lot of care towards himself and all he was experiencing; seeing it all laid out like that gave him perspective—the compassionate kind.

We took a final deep breath together and I thanked him from the bottom of my heart. It was such an honor to go through that process together.

What parts of Jaleel's experience felt familiar—even if your
life circumstances are different? How might that familiarity be
connected to your own identity, history, or circumstances?

Collective wounds: past, present, and future

Jaleel's story shows that collective wounds can manifest in layered, inter-twined ways. The war in Gaza brought him in contact with multiple wounds: sorrow about present day atrocities, complicated feelings about his identity tied to the past, and fear of how things will turn out in the future.

As we continue to look at how collective wounds can manifest, let's do so through the lens of time—organizing them as being related to the present, the past, and future.

This framework makes me think back to the Brett Kavanaugh hearing in 2018, when the Senate Judiciary Committee heard witness testimonies of alleged sexual assault and consequent concerns about his nomination for Supreme Court. The hearing was brutal for me to watch. Hearing the testimony of Christine Blasey Ford, the primary witness who came forward with the accusation, brought up so many deep feelings of rage and despair. *How could someone who so obviously raped that woman be up for nomination?* I held my breath as I watched. *Of course he's not going to be found guilty... they never are.*

The cataclysm of collective wounds was tough to bear. Everyone around me was glued to its coverage. As I doom-scrolled Facebook, post after post either reaffirmed my feelings or sent me deeper into dismay. Either way, it negatively fed the emotional whirlwind that was consuming me.

I was tapped into the collective pain of the current moment—the despair that a person in authority was accused of the heinous act of rape; the idea that we needed a Judiciary Committee hearing to assess his fit for office; and the fact that our government was even considering putting this guy through. Alongside this, I was also feeling collective wounds related to the past—the pervasive sexual violence that has run through society for centuries; the historical failure to protect women and femme people; and the absence of accountability for rape.

I could feel the present-day collective wounds on the surface of my skin, in my pores: a creepy crawly feeling that made me need to take a shower. The wounds related to the past I could feel in my gut, deep in my bones. It was something that couldn't merely be washed off, but that needed my fuller attention.

Present

Collective wounds related to the present are fresh—they're happening in real time, due to events or atrocities unfolding before our eyes. COVID-19, January 6th, Hurricane Katrina, the Texas Uvalde school shooting. These wounds are raw and immediate.

In the Kavanaugh hearing, the present day collective wound was the hearing itself. If I zoom in and look at that current event in a vacuum, outside of historical context, I can see waves of pain rippling out through the collective body. They're relatively small (compared to the long, deep history they're actually related to) but they're clearly there.

The fact that we needed this institutional mechanism to assess whether someone accused of rape should sit on the Supreme Court—that this was even happening—was its own source of collective pain. When I tune into the present day wound alone I feel shock, almost like a smack in the face. It's immediate and visceral.

When working with these types of wounds, the key is to create a healing-centered space that caters to what's happening in real time. Not turning to Instagram or the public square to process what's going on, but spaces where we can slow down, come together in community, and process and understand what's taking place together. These wounds need immediate witnessing—a chance to name the pain as it happens, before it calcifies into something harder to heal.

Past

Collective wounds from the past are the unresolved pain and scar tissue imprinted in our collective memory—wounds from war, persecution, discrimination, state violence, and cultural erasure that got stuck and never properly healed. These are often called historical or intergenerational trauma, passed down across generations like an inheritance nobody asked for.

In the Kavanaugh hearing, these historical wounds were overwhelming. They weren't just my feelings about this one hearing—they were centuries of accumulated rage and grief about patriarchy, about rape culture, and about all the women whose stories were never believed. I could feel these wounds deep in my gut, in my bones. Something ancient and heavy that made me both scream at the top of my lungs and curl up within myself and retreat.

"*If it's hysterical, it's historical*," as somatic abolitionist Resmaa Menakem says.[89] When current events evoke reactions that seem disproportionately large, historical trauma is often at play. The present day event can rip off old scabs, reopening us to wells of historical pain that we may not even know we carry.

When working with collective wounds from the past, we need specialized care and emotionally safe others who understand this terrain. This might look like healing practices within identity-specific spaces, work with family members who share the lineage, or support from therapists skilled in historical trauma.

As Daan van Kampenhout says,

> "…[T]he uncried tears of those who lived before us did not magically disappear after their deaths… [W]e carry all the tears they could not cry during their lifetimes. And when we allow their tears to be cried through us, something is being made whole between the generations, we are engaged in tikkun olam; repairing the world."[90]

Future

Collective wounds related to the future are our anticipatory grief and terror about what's coming. What does the future of democracy look like? Will we be replaced by technology? What happens to the most marginalized as inequality grows? What will a world of 11 billion and counting look like? Terror over resource wars, forced migration, rising sea levels, collapse. Billionaires building bunkers. People faced with visions of apocalypse.

When I was wrestling with the Kavanaugh hearing, part of me was stuck in feelings of dread about the future. *This will never go away*, this part of me thought. Visions of a world forever entrenched in rape culture filled my mind. The future safety of my unborn daughter rang in my ears. These future wounds mingled with the wounds from the past, feeding off each other, sending me down a rabbit hole of despair. I felt hopeless, unsure how to move forward—or if it was even possible to.

The way we feel about the future affects how we are in the present—it shapes how we approach solutions and what we manifest as co-creators of the emerging future. When working with wounds related to the future, we need to feel the full range of what comes up. These fears can reveal what our priorities and values are, and therefore how we can choose to live right now. What am I afraid of losing that I can appreciate more fully today? What's within my circle of control that I can shift to better align with what I want to protect?

Am I using politics as an outlet for personal pain?

Collective healing is a practice of self-awareness—knowing where your personal wounds end and the collective's begin. One of the trickier dynamics to spot is when the heat of politics becomes an outlet for personal pain. In a time when so many collective wounds are active in our collective consciousness—and when political engagement, particularly online, is at an all-time high—it can be hard to notice when our impassioned feelings towards a political issue may be serving as an outlet for a deeper, personal wound that doesn't know how to express itself.

We saw this in Jaleel's story. His heartbreak over the war in Gaza brought forward a much older personal wound: his six-year old self, alone in front of the TV, wondering where the adults were, feeling abandoned and helpless. The pain he felt from the war rippled across and coalesced with the pain from his childhood. Like water droplets on a windshield, the two bled together.

Often, when we feel big emotions about the world, it's because collective wounds are echoing pain we've already carried. For example:

> » If you experienced abuse as a child, police brutality or inhumane prison conditions might stir feelings of being unsafe, overpowered, or neglected

» If you had a domineering parent, figures like Donald Trump or Vladimir Putin might provoke intense reactions tied to those old wounds

» A forest fire halfway across the world can unearth your own buried experience of catastrophic loss

» The frenzied pace of the 24/7 news cycle might amplify the overwhelm already humming in your high-pressure job

When we're emotionally activated by what's happening in the world, one place to begin is to simply acknowledge that the emotional energy we feel might be our own, might be collective, or might be some combination of both. In the midst of strong emotions, we can practice slowing down, grounding into our bodies, and creating a little space between our observing self and what we're feeling. From there, with gentleness and knowing it's not always easy, we can try to identify which parts of our experience are connected to the collective and which might be connected to something personal.

Even slightly uncoupling the current event from our personal history can help us work with these emotional threads more skillfully. By sorting through the wild fog of emotional energy and discerning what is what, we begin to cultivate deeper awareness and more compassionate care:

Think of a moment when you felt emotionally activated by something happening in the world. Let yourself gently stay with those feelings. What do you notice in your body as you bring this to mind?

Can you sense if there's anything layered in what you're feeling— something old, something personal, something inherited, something collective? What part of what you're feeling might be connected to your own story? What part might be tied to something bigger?

Take your time with this, keeping your body grounded as you do. Let the emotional threads speak, one at a time. What do they need? What do you need as you listen?

Listening below the surface

As we've been exploring through Jaleel's story and the past, present, and future framework, understanding collective wounds helps us sort through our own complex emotional responses to the world. We've seen how current events can activate both personal and collective pain, and how learning to discern between them helps us give each part the unique care they need.

But collective wounds also offer us something else: a way to understand other people better, especially those who have wildly different political views than us.

Collective wounds are at the heart of our political narratives—the emotional energy within them drive us to care, to act, to stand on our soapboxes and espouse the truth as we see it. We're all being moved by this energy in different ways; we're just using different stories and worldviews to channel it

This makes me think about my childhood best friend's dad. In one sense, we are very different. But in other senses, we are so much the same. He falls towards the far-right end of the political spectrum (*if we want to still pretend that it's a straight line*)—he was part of the Tea Party Movement, was really into QAnon, and is a big Donald Trump fan. I, on the other hand, swing left—I campaigned for Obama and then Bernie, have worked within institutions like the UN, and I like drag story hours.

I remember sitting with him in a hospital cafeteria, waiting for my best friend's son to be born. Over stale cups of coffee and vending machine egg sandwiches, we talked about the state of the world. Not because either of us planned to, or even really wanted to, but because that's where we both naturally gravitated. It's like we couldn't help ourselves.

The conversation started the way they typically do, in a seemingly banal way, with small talk about life. Then, eventually, without skipping a beat, it started to expand out to include our felt sense about the state of things. Maybe the entry point was a small story about a mutual friend. Maybe it was about rent or the weather. Regardless of its origin, it began to widen into deeper dimensions of what it means to be human these days, especially related to the world.

Here—in this expanded, philosophical space full of suggestive metaphors and words densely packed with meaning—we met each other fully. Energetically, everything we shared made sense. The words he said resonated with the words I said. "*These times are wild, man...*" Or, "*There's a lot going on these days...*" Or, "*Something crazy is brewing.*" There was a shared sense of wonder and awe and excitement and fear and reverence and not knowing between us. We were on the same page, picking up on the same things.

But then, as we began adding context to the felt sense we both shared, things fell apart. As we started rooting what we felt into a story about why it was happening, divergence reared its head and things got ugly. Our on-the-ground understanding of things clashed—the characters who are responsible, the plot of how things are playing out. Like rams butting heads, our ideas clashed and bashed against each other, leaving us both bruised. The tension ballooned. Neither of us was able to hold it, so the energy collapsed and we disconnected.

There was no solid footing we could find—no shared worldview or even facts we could leverage to stay connected. Like so many of us, we got stuck, without any tools to move forward, so instead violently pushed each other away.

In our polarized era, where it seems we're at an intractable stalemate to reach each other, understanding that collective wounds live below the surface of our stories offers a different way forward. If I can support myself to see that underneath even the most ridiculous, heinous, or ludicrous political narratives lies real pain, then I can meet that person there.

It gives me a starting point I can leverage; a way to find common ground. Not because I agree with what they're saying, but because I can relate to what they're feeling. I, too, feel the world's pain. I, too, am channeling collective wounds. If I can identify the specific ones they're feeling, I can meet them there as a fellow feeler. I can meet them there with my heart.

When we recognize that even the most heinous narratives are often powered by some form of pain, it doesn't mean we excuse them. But it does mean we can better understand them. And when we understand, we can get a little bit closer to finding entry points for dialogue, accountability, and even healing.

What's it like to think about collective wounds as a way to gain insight into others? What shifts in you when you consider the idea that beneath political positions, there may be real pain driving them—pain that could be an entry point for connection?

Unmet needs: The roots of collective wounds

Meeting people below the surface of their political stories isn't just about empathizing with their pain—it's also about identifying which collective wounds they're carrying and what universal human needs are crying to be met.

This brings us to another framework for understanding collective wounds—one that looks at collective wounds through the lens of universal human needs.

Why do collective wounds exist? In some ways, this question might seem unnecessary to ask. Collective wounds exist because... something went wrong, people got hurt. We can intuitively answer the question. But human needs theory offers us a more nuanced way of thinking about this.

Human needs theories assert that there are universal basic needs that all humans have. They are the baseline conditions we all require to thrive—things like safety, belonging, dignity, and purpose. They help us understand why people are motivated to do what they do, why conflicts persist. Maslow's Hierarchy of Needs is the most well-known framework.[91] When these needs go unmet on a large scale or over a long period, they leave marks—collective wounds.

Seeing collective wounds as being rooted in unmet human needs deepens our ability to work with them. It deepens the work we're doing to understand ourselves—to understand why certain issues affect us the way they do. It also deepens our ability to connect with others who are politically different—we can relate to unmet human needs as opposed to getting stuck in political narratives.

What have been identified as universal human needs? Let's turn to conflict resolution theorist Sandra Marker's framework that builds on Maslow's work to include needs related to the political and civic dimensions of life.[92]

UNIVERSAL HUMAN NEEDS

Category	Description
Physiological	Food, water, shelter, excretion
Safety & Security	Stable, ordered conditions free from danger or chaos
Belongingness & Love	Acceptance, relational connection
Self-Esteem	Recognition of competence, ability to affect one's environment
Personal Fulfillment	The ability to fully realize oneself in different areas of life
Identity	Having sense of self valued and recognized within the world[93]
Cultural Security	Acknowledgment of one's cultural and religious practices and values
Freedom	Ability to choose and have agency
Justice & Distributive Justice	Equal access to resources and opportunities
Participation	Ability to influence and engage in civic or public life

Collective wounds framework

What follows is a map of different types of collective wounds, each tied to a universal human need. These categories aren't rigid or exhaustive—wounds often overlap—but they can help us make sense of what we're feeling in response to the world.

None of these wounds exist in isolation. There's overlap and interconnectedness between them—for instance, identity-based wounds related to gender can be tied to persecution wounds, as in the Salem Witch Trials. I invite you to explore what follows from an integrative perspective.

As you explore this framework, notice which wounds resonate with you. Maybe certain categories hit you especially hard—injustice, environmental degradation, marginalization. Do wounds related to freedom speak to you in a specific way? Are there ways these themes have showed up in your personal or family life? The wounds that move us often speak to stories and needs in our own lives. This framework isn't just about intellectual clarity— it's an invitation to feel, reflect, and listen within yourself.

UNMET HUMAN NEEDS: COLLECTIVE WOUNDS FRAMEWORK

WOUND TYPE	DESCRIPTION	EXAMPLES	UNMET NEEDS
Injustice			
Identity-based	Systemic and cultural devaluation of people based on race, gender, religion, caste, sexual orientation, disability, or other identity markers.	Jim Crow laws (1877-1965), caste-based discrimination in Indian housing, Don't Ask, Don't Tell (1993-2011)	Identity, safety, belonging, distributive justice
Harm to vulnerable populations	Marginalization, neglect, or abuse of people who require higher levels of care, support, or protection due to age, ability, illness, or structural conditions.	Human trafficking, neglect in elder care homes, abuse in foster care system	Safety, personal fulfillment
Environmental injustice	The disproportionate exposure of marginalized communities to environmental degradation, contamination, and risk due to discriminatory policies, wealth extraction, or neglect.	Flint, Michigan water crisis (2014-2016); Navajo Nation Uranium Mining (1940s-1980s)	Safety, justice, physiological

WOUND TYPE	DESCRIPTION	EXAMPLES	UNMET NEEDS
Violence			
War & conflict	Harm caused by war and armed conflict, often including loss of life, displacement, destruction, and long-term destabilization of societies	World War II, Russia-Ukraine war, ongoing conflict in the Middle East	Safety, physiological
Genocide & ethnic cleansing	Deliberate and systematic elimination or removal of a group (national, religious, ethnic) through violence, force, or coercion	Bosnian War (1992-1995), Rohingya Crisis (2017-present), The Holocaust (1941-1945)	Right to exist / Safety, physiological, belonging, identity, cultural security
Terrorism	Harm caused by acts of terror, whether state-sanctioned or carried out by non-state actors, often resulting in a lack of public safety and psychological terror	September 11th 2001 attacks on the World Trade Center	Safety, identity
State sanctioned violence	Violence deployed by government authorities to assert control, public fear, lack of freedom	Tiananmen Square Massacre (1989), police brutality	Safety, freedom
Domestic abuse & interpersonal violence	Physical, sexual, and psychological abuse in interpersonal or institutional contexts; often silenced or dismissed within dominant culture	Rape culture, violence against women and femme people	Safety, physiological, belonging, self-esteem

WOUND TYPE	DESCRIPTION	EXAMPLES	UNMET NEEDS
Colonial and Authoritarian Systems			
Subjugation, imperialism, colonialism	Imposition of one group's power over another through conquest, colonization, or domination.	British colonization of India, the Scramble for Africa, Indigenous land theft across the Americas	Right to exist / Safety, physiological, belonging, identity, cultural security
Authoritarian rule, dictatorship	Regimes that concentrate power in the hands of a few and restrict civil liberties, political dissent, and public participation.	Chilean Pinochet regime, Stalin's USSR, the Syrian Assad regime	Freedom, participation, justice
Censorship	Suppression of communication, expression, and access to information by authorities.	China's Great Firewall, government-controlled press in Russia, banning LGBTQ+ books or curricula in U.S. school systems	Freedom, participation, justice

WOUND TYPE	DESCRIPTION	EXAMPLES	UNMET NEEDS
Alienation			
Persecution, being exiled	Targeting, oppression, systematic mistreatment, or forced removal of individuals or groups based on their identity, beliefs, or affiliations.	Jewish expulsions during the Spanish Inquisition, the Salem Witch Trials (1692-1693)	Right to exist / Safety, physiological, belonging, identity, cultural security
Cultural erasure	Destruction, suppression, or eradication of languages, traditions, customs, and knowledge systems	Erasure of Kurdish language and identity in Turkey, suppression of Māori practices under British rule in New Zealand	Cultural security, participation, self-esteem, identity
Marginalization	Being on the outskirts of society and therefore not being culturally represented or seen, and having limited political impact	Lack of Indigenous history in narratives about the founding of America; lack of movies or TV shows that represent Hijabis and Muslim women	Cultural security, participation, self-esteem, identity

WOUND TYPE	DESCRIPTION	EXAMPLES	UNMET NEEDS
Economic Harm			
Poverty and structural inequality	Cyclical and inter-generational effects of poverty; lack of access to basic necessities (food, clean water, shelter) and limited or stymied opportunities for economic and social mobility	Urban US poverty, such as the South Side of Chicago; the Dharavi Slum in Mumbai	Physiological, safety, personal fulfillment
Extreme inequality	Widespread and growing disparities in wealth, income and opportunities between groups within countries and across countries	Jeff Bezos's $200 billion net worth compared to the 9% of global population living on less than $2.15 per day	Distributive justice, justice
Unhealthy cultural outcomes of capitalism	Unhealthy or unwanted cultural values shaped by capitalist systems—such as relentless productivity, overconsumption, and commodification of life.	Conspicuous consumption, workaholism and grind culture, celebrity and influencer status tied to wealth and appearance	Personal fulfillment

WOUND TYPE	DESCRIPTION	EXAMPLES	UNMET NEEDS
Environmental Breakdown			
Resource scarcity, famine, drought	Unequal distribution or depletion of natural resources, often due to overconsumption, economic exploitation, or climate shifts.	Cape Town water crisis in South Africa (2015-2020); logging and deforestation of the Amazon Rainforest	Physiological
Natural disasters	Unpredictable, large-scale natural events that damage property, cause loss of life, and disrupt the natural environment	Haiti Earthquake (2010); Hurricane Katrina (2005)	Physiological, safety
Global climate change	Human-induced global warming and long-term alteration of Earth's climate system	Rising sea levels in the Maldives and Pacific Islands, desertification in the Sahel region, record heat waves in Europe and North America	Physiological, safety
Relationship with the Earth	Cultural, personal and spiritual disconnection from the living Earth	Disconnection from ancestral lands, lack of awareness of where food comes from	Personal fulfillment

WOUND TYPE	DESCRIPTION	EXAMPLES	UNMET NEEDS
Institutional Betrayal			
Persistent institutional incompetence, systemic breakdown and failure	The system not responding or delivering the intended results it is designed to.	Delayed federal response during Hurricane Maria in Puerto Rico, public housing failures in New York City (NYCHA mold, heating issues)	Safety
Corruption, misuse of institutional and political power, greed	Unethical or illegal actions by people in power that advance their positions in society	Panama Papers scandal exposing global tax evasion, insider trading	Justice
Lies, lack of trust, lack of transparency	When leaders or institutions withhold, distort, or manipulate the truth.	COVID-19 response and origin of the virus, Vietnam War, Pentagon Papers (1960s-1970s)	Justice

Being a conduit: The role of empaths

Some of us are more naturally sensitive to collective wounds than others. Our passion for a cause doesn't just come from an intellectual belief. It comes from *feeling* the reality of the injustice in the pit of our stomachs, in the layers of our skin, and in the depths of our hearts.

We carry weight we can't always explain. We look around at a world unraveling and wonder: *am I the only one feeling this so deeply?*

If this is you, you're not alone. And you're not defective. You might just be an empath—someone who I see playing a critical role in the times we live in.

Empaths are naturally more sensitive to the subtle dimensions of life than other people. We take in more information, feel things more deeply, and process stimuli more thoroughly than the average person, according to research. Dr. Elaine Aron estimates that 15–20% of people "feel a lot" because we possess a *sensory processing sensitivity* trait,[94] a term she coined based on her decades of scientific research.[95] This type of emotional sensitivity, like all human traits, falls on a spectrum. "Some of us feel a little and some feel a lot," says Hilary Jacob Hendels.

Like I shared earlier, I've always been sensitive. I'm a self-described feeler who has been on a journey of reclaiming what it means to be sensitive for some time now—actively and lovingly peeling away the inherited layers within me that interpret this as a weakness or something to be ashamed of. Instead, I have been exploring the power and strength of my sensitivity to "sense" what's going on at a deeper level. I now see this aspect of myself as a superpower that is able to bring in extra sensory information from my environment. How can that be a bad thing?

Many of us who *feel* the changes going on in the world and see them as a crescendo of crises ricocheting off one another like dominoes might read that last question "How can that be a bad thing?" and respond, "Let me get out my list…"

Feeling the changes in the world can be a mysterious, heavy burden. It's a big ask to see experiences like these as being related to some sort of superpower. This means that some of us are walking tuning forks for the collective emotional field. When others can't (*or won't*) feel the pain of the world, it moves through us instead. As one friend put it: "*It's like 30% of the system is trying to process 100% of the emotional energy.*"

This is not an easy role to play. For some, it results in burnout or despair. For others, it shows up as self-hate, martyrdom, or a chronic sense of being overwhelmed. But what if we could reframe it—not as a flaw, but as a sacred task? What if we understood this not as a burden we have to carry alone, but as an invitation to participate in the healing of the whole?

Within the context of collective healing, I believe we have a powerful and crucial role to play right now. We are being called to lead—even if it's just subtly, in the background—in this time of global heartbreak and collective despair.

To be in relationship with a collective wound is a spiritual calling. It's not something we choose so much as something that reveals itself through who we are and how we've been shaped. Our life experiences—our identities, losses, lineages, and longings—make us uniquely suited to hold particular threads in the collective web. The injustices that stir us most deeply often point to the wounds we are spiritually positioned to tend to. This means that the things that have happened in your life have shaped you in such a way that your architecture is the perfect tuning fork for that thread to reverberate through.

When we work with these wounds, we don't just change ourselves. We also change the field. Each piece we metabolize shifts the system slightly. Each act of feeling becomes an act of service—not because we're fixing the world, but because we're honoring our part in it.

As post-activist philosopher Bayo Akomolafe said in an interview on The Emerald podcast, "*Maybe we are constantly in various degrees in touch with a field that psychology doesn't know how to name… Emotion is not ours, it's not a brain phenomenon. It's a territorial phenomenon. And it enlists bodies in how it comes to matter.*"[96]

If that's true, then maybe what you feel isn't just your pain. Maybe it's the world's pain moving through you, asking to be seen and felt, and thus getting a little closer to being healed. In this case, maybe—just maybe—the work you do to hold it—tenderly, imperfectly, and reverently—is enough to be of healing service to the whole.

What shifts in you when you consider that feeling deeply might be part of your sacred task? What becomes more possible from that place?

Chapter 12

STORIES OF TRANSFORMATION

Welcome to our closing chapter, where we'll look at stories about collective healing. These are stories about real people, whose names and details have been changed to protect their privacy. They have all engaged in collective healing and seen the fruits that came from it. They're fictionalized, based on a compilation of people and communities—but they are real all the same.

The stories show what it looks like to work with collective wounds and feelings related to the world. And not just in an abstract way, but in an on-the-ground, embedded way—through their relationships with family, roles in their jobs, and connection with themselves.

As we've been talking about throughout this workshop-of-a-book, the times we live in are filled with tender and spicy questions. These are the types of questions that have no clear answers. These stories are about people figuring out how to live those questions, in practical, everyday ways.

Spoiler alert—that I don't think you'll be surprised to hear if you've made it this far with me—none of these stories end with a neat, tidy conclusion. None unfold in a linear way. There's no single moment of breakthrough or utopian bliss. Instead, they showcase micro-shifts that came from navigating real-life dynamics and decisions. There are trade-offs, pressures, and limitations. They show how people's inner worlds intersect with outer realities, and the subtle but meaningful change that comes from doing so in a healing-centered way.

Below is a thematic teaser for each story, so you can pick and choose where you want to go:

» Talia and Sarah: war in Gaza, family dynamics
» Kumar: environmental distress
» Brianna: racial dynamics
» Peter: war in Ukraine

The invitation is to read these stories as if you're sitting in Circle with me: noticing what you notice as you read, taking what feels interesting with you and leaving the rest behind.

Talia and Sarah

It was supposed to be a normal Shabbat dinner: just the family, like always. Talia had brought a bottle of wine; her older sister Sarah had baked the challah. The dining room felt warm with ritual and familiarity—candles lit, salad on the table, and their grandfather humming the blessings under his breath.

Talia settled into her chair, her cheeks still sun-kissed from a weekend upstate with friends. She hadn't fully recalibrated to the family's unspoken rules yet—the careful dance around certain topics, and the expectation of nods of agreement. After a year of service work in South America instead of the family-approved Birthright trip, she'd grown accustomed to speaking her mind. Here, though, there were scripts to follow.

As the plates were being passed and the meal was just underway, their grandfather made a comment about the war in Gaza. It was just a passing comment—nothing especially dramatic or surprising. Slightly raising his glass he said, *"Finally, the IDF is doing what needs to be done. L'chaim."*

Talia felt a familiar knot form in her stomach. In this family, statements like that rarely went questioned. The expectation was unspoken but clear: support Israel, full stop. Anything else was betrayal. She glanced at Sarah, who was looking at her plate unphased, and then at her mother, whose smile remained fixed, and unreadable.

She was halfway through pouring a second glass of wine when the words slipped out, almost out of the side of her mouth: *"Right, just bomb our way to peace…"*

A sharp silence fell over the table. Talia immediately regretted speaking, not because she didn't believe what she'd said, but because she knew what would follow. The tension, the disapproval, the subtle ways she'd feel like an outsider for the rest of the night.

Sarah jumped in to soften things. *"No, that's not what he means, it's just that…"*

However, before she could finish, their grandfather cut in. *"Exactly. You understand. It's about survival. We have to be strong."*

"Well, no," Sarah said carefully, *"that's not exactly what I meant…"*

Their mom jumped in abruptly. *"Enough,"* she said. *"No politics at the table. We know where we stand."* She pivoted quickly to serving the roasted chicken, her tone final.

Talia felt herself shrinking in her chair. The conversation moved on around her—aunts discussing a cousin's engagement, her father talking about work—but she remained silent, pushing food around her plate. She caught Sarah looking at her with a mixture of sympathy and frustration. Sarah was the perfect daughter, the peacekeeper: the one who'd done everything right. This wasn't just about politics for Talia. It was about a sense of belonging.

Later that night, after the dishes were done and the family had dispersed, the sisters found themselves alone in the kitchen.

Talia leaned against the counter, arms crossed. *"I just don't get it. You really think all that's going on is fine?"*

Sarah looked up, caught off guard. *"What? No. I was just trying to make sure dinner didn't blow up."*

Talia shook her head. *"You always do that—backpedal into some middle ground that doesn't actually mean anything."*

"That's not fair," Sarah said. *"You act like I'm endorsing everything going on. I was just… trying to keep the peace."*

"At what cost?" Talia's voice rose slightly. *"You sounded like you were agreeing with him. Like you were saying, 'Yeah, maybe bombing civilians is necessary.'"*

"That is not what I meant," Sarah snapped. *"God, Talia, you twist things. I was trying to say it's more complicated than what you made it sound like. You sounded so black-and-white! No context. No history. Just slogans."*

The accusation stung. Talia stared at her. *"Wow."*

"I didn't mean…" Sarah paused.

Talia felt her anger sharpen. *"So what is it then? What do you actually believe?"*

Sarah opened her mouth, then closed it. Her face softened. *"I don't know,"* she admitted. *"I really don't. I just know I can't talk about it in there. And now, apparently, I can't talk about it with you, either."*

They stood there quietly. The painful impasse hung in the air between them, the hum of the refrigerator in the background. Talia felt suddenly exhausted. This wall between them—it wasn't just about Israel and Gaza. It was about all the ways they'd grown apart.

Later that night, Talia lay in bed scrolling through Instagram, unable to sleep. The argument with Sarah kept replaying in her head. She paused on a post from David, a friend from her year abroad who'd been posting thoughtfully about the conflict. He had shared a flyer for an event: "Still Jewish: A space for grief, complexity, and connection."

It wasn't a political meeting or a rally, but a space created specifically for Jews grappling with what was happening—a place to tend to the weight of this moment and the complicated layers of what it meant to be Jewish right now. David had added his own comment: *"Finally found a space where I don't have to check parts of myself at the door."*

Talia stared at the post for a long time. She felt a longing so acute it was almost physical—for a place where she could speak honestly without being labeled a traitor or naive. Somewhere that she could hold her love for her Jewish identity alongside her horror at what was happening in Gaza. A place where she could admit she felt lost.

After a moment's hesitation, she took a screenshot and texted it to Sarah.

"Thinking of checking this out next weekend. Might be different from the usual 'dialogue' spaces."

Sarah's response came quickly: *"Not sure. Remember that campus thing last year? Where the speaker compared Zionism to white supremacy? I felt so out of place—no one cared that I have family in Tel Aviv."*

Talia sighed. She remembered. She thought about how Jewish communities have long stood at the forefront of progressive movements. But recently, many felt abandoned—left reeling by the rise in antisemitism and the silence of their supposed allies.

She also remembered the forum at the Jewish Community Center where people had said all the right things about nuance and dialogue, but you could tell which answers were acceptable before anyone even spoke.

She typed back, *"Yeah, I get it. I'm skeptical too. But David vouched for it, and... I don't know. I'm tired of feeling like I don't fit in anywhere. Maybe this is different?"*

Three dots appeared, disappeared, then appeared again. Finally, *"OK. I'll go. But if it's weird, I'm out."*

They arrived at an unassuming brownstone near the park. There was a small paper sign on the door with the event's name, along with, "Buzz for the 3rd Floor." As they climbed the stairs, Talia could hear the murmur of voices above.

The room was quiet when they walked in. There was a circle of chairs, and some soda and snacks on the side. Talia scanned the faces, surprised by the diversity—young and old, some wearing kippot, others clearly secular like herself. There were no protest signs, no Israeli flags, and no clear markers of which "side" this gathering represented.

The facilitator, Miriam—a woman with kind eyes and silver-streaked hair—welcomed them and helped them find a seat. Talia and Sarah sat side by side, both feeling tense. Talia noticed Sarah checking the exits, clearly planning her escape route, and almost smiled despite her own nervousness.

After everyone settled, Miriam introduced herself. *"I started these gatherings after October 7th,"* she explained, *"when I found myself unable to speak honestly in any of the spaces I belonged to. My background in conflict resolution put me in touch with people doing similar work in Israel and Palestine, and I kept hearing the same thing from American Jews—that there was nowhere to be whole."*

She looked around the circle. *"If you're feeling confused, you're not alone. So many of us have been struggling to find somewhere—anywhere—where we can express what we're really thinking. Every space seems to demand we pick a side, that we be all one thing or another. There's no room for grief, for doubt, for holding multiple truths at once. And that absence—that's its own kind of loss, isn't it? So that's why we're here. To sit in that messiness together."*

Talia felt something loosen in her chest. She glanced at Sarah, who was staring intently at Miriam, her expression unreadable.

One by one, people began to speak. A young man talked about his love for Israel—and how that love felt tested every time he turned on the news. A mother whose friend's son was among the hostages taken by Hamas spoke through tears about her constant worry and the pain of feeling like some people forget about the hostages still being held. A woman described her fear of rising antisemitism and how it had closed her off from people around her. Someone shared the shame they felt over their silence. Another told a story about their last trip to Jerusalem, before the war, and how complicated it had felt even then.

Talia listened, stunned by how familiar each story felt, even when the politics expressed differed from her own. These were people holding grief for Palestinians alongside love for Israel; concern about antisemitism alongside criticism of the ongoing conflict. Throughout it all, there was a common thread—how the loneliness of not fitting cleanly into any one narrative was its own kind of pain.

When it was her turn, Talia surprised herself with what came out.

"I feel like I'm living two lives," she said. *"In one, I'm the family radical, the one who questions Israel's military response, who cares 'too much' about Palestine. In the other, I'm not radical enough—I still feel deeply connected to being a Jew, I still care about Jewish safety, and I still believe Israel has a right to exist."*

She felt her voice catch. *"I'm tired of being pushed to choose a side, when all I want is to choose peace. I want the hostages home and the bombing to stop. I can condemn Hamas without condemning all Palestinians. I don't want to be right; I just want to not feel crazy. I don't know what peace looks like in practice, but I believe in it wholeheartedly, and I want it for everyone."*

As she spoke, Talia realized it'd been a while since she tried putting words to what she thought—with all its contradictions and uncertainties. It felt like exposing a tender, guarded part of herself—one she was forever trying to understand. There was a vulnerability in voicing these half-formed thoughts, but also a strange relief.

From across the circle, an older woman put her hand on her heart and nodded in resonance. It felt like she was saying, "*It's exhausting, isn't it?*"

Talia blinked back tears.

Later, much to Talia's surprise, Sarah spoke too. She talked about her trips to Israel, and her connection to the land, but also her increasing horror at the government's actions. She spoke about feeling abandoned by progressive spaces that seemed to have no room for her Jewish identity or her complicated feelings about Israel.

"*I feel like I'm failing, both at being a good Jew and a good person,*" Sarah said, voice breaking. "*And I don't know what to do with that.*"

Talia watched her sister cry openly in a room full of strangers and felt a rush of love so strong it took her breath away. She reached for Sarah's hand without thinking, and Sarah gripped it tightly.

In that moment, Talia saw it clearly: they were different in how they spoke and what they emphasized, but beneath it all was the same yearning—for safety, for dignity, and for a world where no one's pain had to be denied to affirm another's. They didn't need to agree to recognize that in each other.

They left that first meeting with more questions than answers, but also with a sense of relief. Something in them had been seen and heard.

"*Do you want to get coffee?*" Sarah asked as they walked to the subway, the winter sun low in the sky.

"*Yeah,*" Talia said. "*I'd like that.*"

Over lattes in a crowded café, they talked—really talked—for the first time in months. About their fears and hopes. About their grandfather's trauma and how it shaped him. About what it meant to be Jewish in this moment. They didn't solve anything; they didn't even fully agree, but something had shifted between them.

"*I'm going back next week,*" Talia said as they were getting ready to leave. "*To the gathering.*"

Sarah nodded. *"I'll come too."*

And she did. Week after week, they returned to that circle. The space became a kind of anchor for Talia. An island of coherence in a sea of noise. She found herself bringing questions there that she couldn't ask anywhere else.

The changes were subtle at first. Talia had always known where her grandfather's views came from—rooted in profound trauma, shaped by the loss of friends on October 7th and the fear that never quite left. But she found herself listening differently now: not always to agree, but to understand more fully what it meant to have that kind of history. She started a group chat with cousins her age who she suspected might share some of her questions. She began attending services at a progressive synagogue, reconnecting with ritual in a way that felt authentic.

The biggest change was between her and Sarah. They still disagreed, but now they could talk about it without shattering their connection. They'd learned to speak from the heart, to listen without interrupting, and to stay present when discomfort arose.

Six months later, Talia found herself facilitating a youth circle at her synagogue, creating the kind of space Miriam had created for her but for teenagers. As she arranged chairs in a circle, Talia thought about all the healing that remained to be done—in her family, in the Jewish community, and in Israel-Palestine. The work was nowhere near finished. But at least now she wasn't doing it alone.

Talia's story reminded me how essential collective healing spaces are—especially in times of profound division and pain. These spaces aren't about erasing differences or demanding agreement; they're about making room for the full emotional and political spectrum of our situations. It reminds me that we don't need to have all the answers to facilitate healing. Sometimes the most important thing we can offer is simply a place to be in the questions together.

Kumar

Kumar had been carrying the weight of the world for a long time. Not in any heroic way—more in a quiet, grinding way. It was the kind of low-grade despair that lives just behind the eyes, coloring everything you see.

It came from knowing too much. About the climate. The systems. And the stakes. How runaway climate change has the potential to trigger a cascade of effects, leading to the collapse of industrial societies as we know them. A fear that kept him up late at night.

He didn't talk about it much, but it was always there—the existential fear. He cared about the planet. He had actually trained as an environmental scientist, before pivoting to a more stable tech job after his daughter Maya was born. These days he did remote work for a local health network—decent pay and decent hours, with flexibility to co-parent; but nowhere near the kind of work he had once dreamed of doing.

There's a simultaneous brittleness and density to what Kumar was carrying. One day, on the go after Maya's soccer practice, he tossed an empty bag of chips into the park bin on their way out. As the bag left his hand, his imagination transported him to a landfill where that plastic bag would sit for hundreds of years. In the blink of an eye, he saw thousands of these bags being thrown away each day. And that was just in his own country. As his mind moved outward into the rest of the world, the immensity of waste we're collectively generating rocked him to his core. He started to spiral.

The wave came fast. Guilt. Self-hate. The feeling that he was the problem. That his life—his apartment, his commute, his compromises—was part of everything that was wrong. A similar suffocating feeling took over. He felt trapped, stuck in a system he didn't want to participate in. A system that didn't reflect his values and instead threatened the very things he cared about most.

"What should I do?" he thought to himself anxiously. *"Hoard all of the bags I use?"* His tiny apartment could only handle so much. *"Never buy anything that comes in a bag?"* He tried. He composted. He brought reusable bags. He bought bulk when he could. But when life got overwhelming—work running late, during Maya's after-school pickup, or grabbing groceries between meetings—he caved. And every time he did, it felt like a failure.

In moments like this, he'd find himself daydreaming about running off to an eco-village somewhere in the mountains. Living off the land. Growing his own food. Everything smelling like soil and sun. People gathered at long wooden tables, contemplating life. Things would be simpler, aligned. He could feel it.

And then—he was snapped back. The fluorescent lighting in his backroom office strained the tops of his eyes. A blinking Teams notification barked for his attention. The reality of life—his year-long lease, his ex-wife's shared custody—came into view and the daydream subsided. He couldn't run. Not really.

What began to shift for Kumar wasn't anything dramatic. The low-grade despair had been with him for so long, just living in the background, that it took time for things to shift. However, one time, coming down on the other side of this fantasy, a quiet realization started to peak through—the eco-village fantasy wasn't just about escape. It was pointing him toward something. Yes, it was pointing towards his values: regeneration, connection, interdependence. But it also pointed towards a feeling—a connectedness in his body, a vitality tied to nature, and a sense of belonging with other people who care.

And while he couldn't go off-grid, he could bring some of that spirit into his life now. He could recognize where this already existed and build on it—where the eco-village way of life was already present in his life. Teaching Maya how to grow herbs on the windowsill. Pausing to thank the Earth before throwing something away. Noticing shifts that come with the moon phases.

None of this was a silver bullet solution, but it softened something. It helped him begin to peel back layers and unlocked new places to go within himself when he started slipping into a spiral. He got deeper into history, learning about how different peoples across the world have lived through upheaval. He realized that the risk of collapse isn't new. People across time—including in his own bloodline—had faced loss of what they knew and found ways to carry on. His own grandparents had grown food out of necessity, and some of that wisdom lived in him too. That doesn't necessarily make it easier. But it means there's a lineage—something he could tap into—and he wasn't alone.

Kumar's story reminded me that sometimes collective wounds don't shout. They press and build. And they leave us feeling like we're never enough. But when we stop to feel what's underneath the despair—what it's protecting, what it's pointing to—we can start to reclaim a sense of agency. Not in fixing the whole system. But in how we live inside it.

Brianna

At work, Brianna liked chatting with customers. She worked at a neighborhood health food store, the kind of place with organic produce, hand-written signs, and a familiar rhythm to the customers. Brianna liked being part of that rhythm. She liked chatting with people while bagging groceries or restocking tea. There was something grounding about the brief but real connections she got to have throughout the day—little windows into other people's lives.

But she had started to notice something off in her interactions with some of the customers—specifically, certain white women. They'd stammer, or stumble over their words. Their voices would change when speaking with her. It wasn't every time, but enough that it stuck with her. She could feel a kind of tension—as if they were tripping over something inside themselves.

At first, Brianna brushed it off. *Everyone gets nervous sometimes,* she thought. But it kept happening. And it wasn't happening with her other coworkers, or with the older Jamaican man who worked at the register next to hers. It was only happening with her.

It wasn't until it kept happening that she began to connect the dots. They were second-guessing themselves—overthinking something. And it was something about her—being in a Black body, in this social moment—that was triggering that.

When it first clicked, she was pissed. These weren't overtly racist interactions. But something was being projected onto her—something she hadn't asked for. It felt like they were caught in some sort of internal racial confusion guilt loop, and she was the screen it was playing out on.

She didn't want to be someone else's mirror. She didn't want people's anxiety about their whiteness put on her. She hadn't asked for that. She was just trying to connect—to be herself, and to have a normal, human interaction.

It wasn't just frustrating. It hurt, because Brianna loved connecting with people—her parents had raised her to see the beauty in others, to be curious and open, and to know she belonged everywhere—everyone does. She'd spent her whole life learning and practicing feeling comfortable in predominantly white spaces. And now, somehow, that comfort was being knocked out of balance—not by hostility, but by a kind of self-consciousness.

Even worse, it started to affect her behavior. She found herself avoiding certain customers, shortening conversations. She was pulling back from the very thing that gave her joy. And that jumble of emotions—frustration, pity, confusion, and fatigue—started to pile up.

There was one moment, she told me, that really stayed with her. She felt bad for one of the women—genuinely bad. *"She looked so uncomfortable. I just wanted to say, like, it's okay! You don't have to try so hard. Just be normal."* But that compassion came tangled up with resentment. Because she remembered her own years of being hyper-aware of how she spoke—of trying to get it "right" in white spaces. Now she was on the receiving end of a dynamic that mirrored parts of her past in a way that felt completely upside down.

What helped her was talking with an old friend—someone she'd known since high school, who understood her and didn't need everything explained. Her friend shared some of what she'd been seeing in her own circles: the way progressive white folks, especially women, were trying so hard to be racially literate that they were tying themselves in knots. *"They're trying so hard not to mess up,"* her friend said, *"that they're kind of... messing up."*

That conversation helped her name something bigger—this wasn't just about a few customers at a grocery store. It was part of a larger collective wound around race—especially between white and Black people; white and Black women in particular. It was a dynamic that was creating a kind of feedback loop, keeping everyone stuck in patterns they were trying to move beyond.

Brianna didn't excuse it, but she understood it. And that understanding helped her disentangle what had gotten all knotted up inside her. The dynamic she was witnessing wasn't just personal. It was part of a larger cultural wound—one that left some people feeling awkward about how to relate across racial differences.

That didn't mean she had to carry it. But it meant she could notice when it was present and meet it differently.

Rather than bracing for the discomfort or retreating from it, Brianna started to stay. Not to fix or soothe the other person—but to remain steady in herself. She let her own clarity be the ground beneath her feet when someone else was spinning. She found herself offering a kind of quiet reassurance in those moments—not aloud, but inwardly: *"You're okay. I'm okay. We're alright."*

That simple shift changed her days. She still felt the tension sometimes. However, it didn't throw her off or keep her from doing her thing.

Brianna taught me that part of collective healing is learning how to hold the complexity of a moment without letting it define you. Sometimes that means feeling the projection, recognizing it for what it is, and still choosing to stay open—not because you owe anyone anything, but because it's part of who you are and what you value, which in her case was connection.

The truth is that collective wounds like this show up in relationships all the time. Whether it's between people of different generations, political leanings, religious backgrounds—or, more often than not, some layered combination of these things. We can so easily become avatars to each other these days, subconsciously projecting assumptions or stories onto each other.

Brianna did the beautiful work that is collective healing: she created space for the complicated things she was feeling, and made sure they didn't get in the way of her being who she wanted to be in the world. That's what collective healing makes possible. It is not that the collective wounds disappeared, but they don't get to be the one driving the interaction. She does.

Peter

"Breaking news." The notification flashes across Peter's phone. "Russia invades Ukraine." His heart stops. War has broken out—the kind he and many others have been fearing for years.

The world watches in horror, and Peter, an American with family ties to the region, can't look away either. He finds himself racing through article after article, trying to stay on top of all that is happening. What is happening on the ground? How are people responding? He imagines people like his loved ones scrambling to figure out what to do. What would *he* do?

The seeking network of his brain is firing on high. Searching, searching, searching... for what? He doesn't totally know. He finds himself cycling between tabs, compulsively refreshing his feed, checking WhatsApp, and translating Telegram updates. It takes him over: first thing in the morning until last thing at night, and every waking moment in between—looking for casualty reports, real-time reactions, on-the-ground videos. Anything he can get his hands on. If he can just find what he is looking for—a place to land—he might have a fuller picture of what's taking place.

He feels a sense of duty within it all—a responsibility to stay informed. His heart is being pushed and pulled by this duty—the drive to act, to take up arms, to defend. He feels pummeled by the crippling reality of being so helpless and so far away.

He wonders how to slow down within it all—how to be in his body. "*It's actually too painful to be there...*" he sighs. A familiar buzz of dissociation hums in his ears as he keeps powering through.

Eventually it becomes too much. The weight of it all—the fear, helplessness, and information overload—reaches a tipping point and he crashes. Needing to take the day off work, he lies in bed and grieves. His nervous system does for him what he couldn't do for himself—forcing him to rest.

his forced staycation leads him to do what he's always done when life becomes too much. He shuts off, binges old episodes of *The Simpsons*, and indulges in a box of doughnuts. In times past—especially when scary things were happening in the world—he'd go through a similar cycle: hyperactivation, spinning his wheels, burning out, and then not looking back. But this time around he can't do that.

"I've gotta do something different..." Peter thinks, late into the afternoon. *"This shit's too important."* His personal ties to the conflict mean he can't let this one go.

He begins by taking the rest of the day off from the news. He gives himself whatever time and space he needs before dipping a toe back in.

And for Peter, this is his first step toward bringing more awareness into what he's doing. He wants to make sure he doesn't slip into avoidant mode—and also that he doesn't fall right back into taking things in from a place of addictive urgency.

So he closes his eyes and takes a deep breath before reopening his news feed, checking in with himself, ever so briefly. It seems small, this check-in, but it's actually big. It's him using that nanosecond to reclaim a connection with himself. It is a step towards making sure he's taking in the news, but that the news isn't taking over him.

He begins to see his experiences of dissociation differently. Like it's a threshold. An internal alarm system. His body and mind saying: *WEE-OO WEE-OO. Back up. You've gone too far.*

He notices when he becomes dizzy, glossing over entire paragraphs, feeling distant, like he's hovering above what he sees. As opposed to when he feels present, able to really take in what's in front of him, making sense of each piece as he goes.

He starts noticing the physical cues that he's nearing his edge—a tightness in his scalp, a kind of internal buzzing. And rather than overriding them, he returns to that nanosecond check-in—letting out a heavy *"huhhh"* that brings him back to himself.

"It seems counterintuitive," he tells me, *"but I can actually get more when I take in less. Sure, I miss stuff—updates and news alerts or whatever. But what I do take in, I can really absorb. It makes me more connected to what's happening and able to do something about it from a better place."*

A few months later, when Ukrainian families began arriving in his city through the humanitarian parole program, Peter knew exactly how he wanted to help. He signed up as a volunteer interpreter at the local resettlement agency. Every Tuesday, he'd spend his afternoon helping families navigate the maze of paperwork—social security applications, school enrollments, medical forms.

The work required presence. He couldn't zone out or dissociate when a mother was explaining to a doctor why her eight-year-old suddenly couldn't speak—"*after the sirens,*" she'd say simply. Or when he had to translate a father's work history, listening as the man listed his credentials as an engineer before adding, "*but I can do any work here, cleaning is fine.*"

These weren't headlines or statistics—they were people sitting across from him, carrying the war in their bodies, trusting him to bridge two worlds. The work he did to help himself digest what was happening and have agency in how he shows up helped him to do that.

Peter's story speaks to something subtle yet powerful that collective healing offers. He found a way to have choice and agency in a situation that he had little to no control over, but which affected him deeply. He began making choices that gave him greater agency over himself and his internal world—not just for his own well-being, but also for how he could show up and respond to the conflict.

Instead of hiding away in avoidance, he learned how to work with his overwhelm and the way the media landscape feeds it, in order to stay present with something important to him. And in doing so, he began to recover something essential: his capacity to stay with what's real, without losing himself in the process, and then to translate that into volunteer work that meant a lot to him.

Where did you see yourself reflected in these stories? Was it in a feeling someone had? A struggle they named? A shift they moved through? Which story felt furthest from your life—but still resonated somehow? What part of you responded?

What does this chapter make you wonder about your own story? What have you been carrying, feeling, and holding on behalf of something larger? If your story were included in this chapter, what themes would it explore

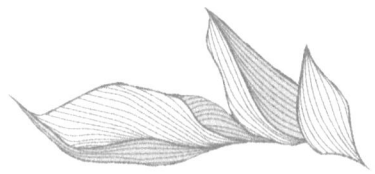

CLOSING THE CIRCLE

Wow, here we are—at the end of the book. Blowing out the candle and closing our time together with a final heart connection.

In alignment with the Circle practice I've come to know and love, I offer the energy conjured within this book, between you and me and all who read it, to that which is greater than ourselves, whatever that means to each of us. I'm doing that for myself personally right now.

I want to close by acknowledging you and all you are: all the etches and grooves, contours and lines that make up your unique architecture. All that makes you uniquely positioned to be of service, especially healing service, to the world in the way that you are. Thank *you* for this. You have a specific and distinct role to play. And the world is so blessed to have you here to play it.

Placing my feet fully on the floor. Breathing into the lowest part of my belly. Resting my attention inward to notice what I notice, and pausing here, I invite you into these final questions in closing:

> » *Think back to the beginning of this book, when you first picked it up and checked in with yourself. Check in with yourself now. What may have changed or shifted after reading this book? What within you has stayed the same?*
> » *What are you taking home with you because it resonated so clearly, so deeply? What are you taking home with you because it didn't? Because it left you with something to mull over and tend to so you can see what arises?*

From my heart to yours, from my home to yours— thank you.

APPENDIX

A. Gentle Encouragements

A few gentle suggestions for how to go about reading this book:

Continuously return to yourself

Practice staying connected to yourself as you go about the book. Notice your body, your emotional landscapes, personal edges, and your intuition as you read.

Notice resonance

When your own emotions or bodily sensations respond to what you read. Maybe it's a story or a specific line. A spark fills your chest, or a heaviness sinks into your legs. You might place a hand on your heart or pause to take a breath when something lands. This is your body's wisdom responding. Let it be part of the mix.

Use everything here to deepen your awareness

Notice your energy and attention as you read. What brings you to life? What shuts you down? What leaves you feeling in between? Stay curious. Use everything you experience to get to know yourself better.

Trust where you're drawn

There's no one way to read this. Trust where you feel called to go. Skip around. Skim. Linger. Re-read. Trust how you're guided to read.

Expect not to resonate with it all

This book is a humble offering—just one grain of sand in a big beach of ideas. Some things might not land for you—and that's okay. Let everything here be an invitation, not a must. Even the parts that don't resonate can be useful—as a springboard to clarify your own truth, position, and role.

Move at the speed of your slowest part

Maybe one part of you is eager to move forward, while another needs time. Give precedence to the slower one. Let it take the lead. There may be something there that needs a little more space.

B. How I identify

As we as a world continue to make more space for all of the rich, beautiful diversity that exists on our planet, it's necessary for me to share and own the histories, realities, privileges, and inequities that I've experienced, and how they fit into the larger puzzle of our collective body.

Being clear and open about who I am, the body I inhabit, and the vehicle through which I offer things feels important in the pursuit of co-creating an inclusive, conscious world. I hope it also builds greater trust with you as a reader.

I also look at this as a practice. A practice of acknowledging differentiation as a gesture towards reconciliation and collective healing. Just as with all spiritual practices, once the technique is practiced enough times it becomes integrated into the practitioner's psyche, spirit, and consciousness in a way that allows the practice to fall away. No longer needing to be done so explicitly; instead, it is inherently embedded.

This is my hope for this practice, too: that we collectively move towards a place where we've practiced acknowledging identity enough times that we can let it fall away and move towards a new phase of relating to each other that still celebrates our differences, and further liberates us from the constraints that identity boxes impose.

My lived experience is through the body of a white (mainly of Irish, German, and Polish descent), cis-gender woman born into a middle-class family in the suburbs of Pennsylvania. My lived experience is through a body that's sensitive to energy, emotions, touch, and the cycles of nature. My lived experience is social, outgoing, in the world; as well as introspective, contemplative, reflective.

My lived experience at a foundational level is from a home of love, as well as a home of addiction and pain. I honor my family, my lineage, my ancestors; and the resources and challenges embedded within us. They are my biggest teachers.

My lived experience through choice is one of spiritual seeking, multicultural connection, and service; full of learning, color, and Guidance. My lived experience is queer as a bi/pansexual human, and transcendental of form, as a spiritual being having a human experience.

My spirituality is rooted in Christianity and the Christian lineage given to me by my family. It is rooted in nature, naturalness, and feminine cycles gifted to me by the Earth. And universalism, interconnectedness, and an understanding that there are many rivers to the ocean of God, gifted to me by the times we live in.

I'm Lila's mom and Anees' wife. I'm not sure if I prefer the term wife or life partner—I think soul mate's probably better than either. These two people mean everything to me, and I'm so grateful to be together. Anees is a healing-centered psychiatrist and psychotherapist, so there's a lot of nerdy healing pillow talk in our house.

My professional experience is in international sustainable development and sociology. I like to be practical, using applied social science and a whole-systems approach to figure out how to address things like poverty, gender inequality, and climate change.

I live in NYC, an international city surrounded by all sorts of different, beautiful people. It's part of my practice of building the world I want to see more of in the future, with integrated multiculturalism, and a sense of co-existence.

My lived experience has parameters to it that do not make it universal. I would say it has limitations, but I don't believe it needs to be viewed that way. Instead, I am trusting in the puzzle pieces we're all provided with. My lived experience does not hold wisdom or medicine for everyone. It's not meant to. In the name of inclusivity and plain ol' common sense, my lived experience is but one tiny perspective in a vast sea of rich, wise vantage points.

What does your story hold?

I own and recognize that I embody privileges and social truths that exist in our fractured, unequal world. I own and recognize my privilege as a white body of European descent in this world that historically prioritizes the lives of those with lighter skin tones. I own and recognize the socio-emotional luxury that comes with being born into a body that I identify with. I own and recognize the psychological ease that comes with having socioeconomic safety nets. I own and recognize the political freedoms I'm privileged to have as an American.

I recognize that my life is a combination of happenstance and hard work. I am a product of the structures that be, as well as the choices and sacrifices of my family. I am also the result of my own hard work and dedication, as well as God's unique path for me.

I welcome and invite voices forward to balance mine, to fill in gaps, to create more wholeness, and to build a multidimensional resonance. My request is that any voices do so in a way that is respectful, self-aware, and done with a vision of interdependence.

I commit and recommit my life to breaking abusive patterns, ending oppressive cycles, and liberating the God-given potential of our interconnected world. I welcome this as messy, humble work.

My offerings are my consciousness, are my healing, are my personal journey.

May it be of service.

C. Guidelines For Listening & Sharing

It is important to establish a space where everyone takes their intention to share and to listen with compassion seriously. Nothing that is shared is unimportant, stupid, wrong, or abnormal. Everyone is welcome to share. No one should feel pressured to.

When sharing our stories, we speak from our own personal experiences. We use "I/me statements" and are mindful not to generalize or make assumptions about others when sharing.

After someone has finished sharing, we refrain from responding directly to them or engaging in cross-talk. We do not give unsolicited advice, interrogate, debate, criticize, control, or dominate.

We ask that you respect the confidentiality of each person in the Circle. We ask that what you see here, what is said here, when you leave here, let it stay here.

These Guidelines were originally developed as part of the NYC chapter of the climate movement Extinction Rebellion's "Extinction Recovery" support program for members, and informed by tools used within Centering Prayer community practice.

D. Collective Healing Lineages and Landscape

Ever since I hung up my virtual "OPEN" sign for We Heal For All and stepped into the work of collective healing, I've had the pleasure of meeting people from all walks of life who are drawn to it. These have ranged from a Ugandan public health professional envisioning a spiritual dimension to the UN's Sustainable Development Goals, to a Brazilian climate activist naming her grief for the first time, and to a U.S.-based facilitator supporting Indigenous youth on the frontlines—each person shared a felt resonance with the idea of collective healing. And each expressed that resonance in a way that was uniquely their own.

When someone new approaches me about collective healing, there's often this electric quality to our conversations. Sparks of creative energy fly between us as we put words to the felt sense we share. It's like a homecoming of sorts, to find a fellow trailblazer who's also sniffing out this untapped path. The feeling of being kindred spirits is high. Colleagues within the same field of practice! We're exchanging ideas, on the same page, until... it becomes clear we're talking about entirely different things.

Yes, this happens time and time again—I'll be riffing with someone on collective healing when it becomes clear we're talking about quite different things. I love it when this happens because it gives me a chance to practice articulating the specific form of collective healing I feel called to, while learning how the term is being used more widely across the field.

I see collective healing as an emergent field of practice and inquiry—meaning it's taking shape as we go. It doesn't have a long, established history being disseminated top-down through universities. Instead, it's being born from the ground up through community groups, organizations, and activists responding to needs in real time. It's being brought into form by those of us who feel the deep need for it or the raw pulse of what it could be. It is as if it's a gift from the Universe asking to come through, and we're each a different facet of how it might arrive.

That's why it's important to name that collective healing has many faces. And because this term is at the center of this book, it helps to take a look at the wider landscape it exists within. What follows is a high-level orientation to the larger field and its lineages—an ecology of the collective healing field, if you will. A glimpse into some of the ways people use the term, and the diverse approaches and meanings it has across different communities, contexts, and lineages:

Collective Healing Ecosystem

» **Indigenous spiritual traditions**, where personal and collective spiritual health are understood to be interconnected—the community itself has a soul that requires care. Siberian shamans heal social rifts through divination and ancestral communion,[97] while Diné medicine people perform ceremonies like the Blessingway to restore balance to the cosmos, and therefore the community.[98]

» **Contemporary spiritual and religious**, where modern practitioners like the Zen Peacemakers host annual Bearing Witness retreats at Auschwitz-Birkenau, where multi-faith participants bear witness to humanity's capacity for both harm and healing.[99] Then there is Daan van Kampenhout, who combines shamanism with family constellation work in "Systemic Ritual" to address collective and ancestral patterns.[100]

» **Contemporary transdisciplinary work**, which weaves together insights from psychology, spirituality, and systems thinking. Joanna Macy's Work That Reconnects helps people transform environmental despair into active hope through grief work and deep interconnection with all life.[101] Thomas Hübl's Pocket Project focuses on integrating collective trauma through relational presence and somatic awareness.[102] Meanwhile, somatic practices, such as those taught by Staci K. Haines,[103] center the body as a site of transformative justice and embodied leadership.

» **Liberation movements**, where healing practices have been central throughout history, and have often emerged in response to collective trauma and oppression. The Civil Rights Movement used prayer circles, storytelling, and freedom songs to sustain activists fighting racism and state violence.[104] During the 1980s

AIDS epidemic, LGBTQ+ communities created support groups and memorial marches that both healed community grief and advocated for desperately needed civil liberties and healthcare access.[105] Present-day Healing Justice extends this lineage, advanced by collectives like Kindred Southern Healing Justice, explicitly making the connection between healing and justice in movement work and beyond.[106]

» **Scholarly and practitioner-based trauma frameworks**, like Dr. Maria Yellow Horse Braveheart's work on historical trauma, which identified how genocide and colonization create lasting psychological and spiritual wounds in Native communities.[107] Dr. Joy DeGruy's research on Post Traumatic Slave Syndrome links systemic violence against Black Americans to intergenerational trauma and ongoing psychological harm, while mapping pathways toward healing.[108] There are contemporaries like Resmaa Menakem and the work of somatic abolitionism.[109] And there is the growing field of climate psychology, spearheaded by associations like the Climate Psychology Alliance, which offers research and tools for working with ecological grief and anxiety.[110]

» **Intergroup healing initiatives** address conflict, systemic violence, and communal harm through structured processes. South Africa's Truth and Reconciliation Commission[111] and Rwanda's National Unity and Reconciliation Commission[112] created platforms for national truth-telling between victims and perpetrators.

» **Community healing** in the U.S., community policing and restorative justice programs work to rebuild trust between marginalized communities and law enforcement.[113] These forms of collective healing pursue repair through dialogue, education, and policy at institutional and societal levels.

The field is broad and transdisciplinary. It touches everything from interpersonal neurobiology to public policy. From mindfulness to mutual aid. From cultural revival to systems change. This appendix doesn't capture the full breadth of it. Instead, it honors the vastness of what exists, points toward some of its lineages, and clarifies the lens I'm working through in this book.

I'm wondering what you would add?

Types of Healing: A Working Framework

Healing is a big, layered word. It can refer to anything from the mending of a bone to the mending of a society. To help us get our bearings, I will organize healing into three broad categories: **individual**, **relational**, and **collective**. These overlap and influence one another. None exists in isolation. But thinking in these terms can help us locate the different scales and methods of healing work.

The following table outlines this framework in more detail.

A note on interconnectedness: Though separated here for clarity, these forms of healing are deeply interwoven. Collective wounds show up in families. Relational ruptures live in the body. Personal healing can ripple outward into cultural shifts. So, as you explore this framework, hold it lightly. Let it support your understanding, not box it in.

TYPES OF HEALING: FRAMEWORK

Type	Subtype	Description
Individual	Physical healing	Addresses imbalances or wounds in the body (e.g., injury, illness, chronic pain).
	Emotional & psychological healing	Focuses on mental/emotional challenges (e.g., anxiety, depression, stress).
	Spiritual healing	Involves healing existential or spiritual disconnection (e.g., purposelessness).
	Energy healing	Works with subtle energy systems to promote balance and well-being.
Relational	Interpersonal healing	Heals harm or disconnection between two people (e.g., couples, friends).
	Family healing	Supports healing within family systems and generational dynamics.
	Community-based healing	Facilitates repair within small communities (e.g., restorative justice).
Collective	Intergenerational & ancestral healing	Heals wounds passed down through generations due to war, famine, or trauma.
	Historical trauma healing	Addresses shared trauma within a group due to historical events (e.g., genocide).
	Systemic trauma healing	Targets wounds from systemic oppression or institutional failure.
	Community-based healing	Supports communities after crises (e.g., natural disasters, mass violence).
	Cultural healing	Reclaims subjugated languages, traditions, or cultural identities.
	Inter-group healing	Facilitates healing between groups after conflict or injustice.
	Earth-based healing	Repairs disconnection from nature through spiritual or ecological practices.

E. Emotions and The Change Triangle

Emotions like:

Safety

Emotions like safety. For it to be psychologically, socially, and physically safe for them to be shared. They won't be judged or used against a person. They will be seen and accepted. Safety can come from another person or from a group. It can also come from yourself, in how you internally respond and react to your own emotions.

To be validated

Emotions like to be understood. Even if you don't agree with what a person is saying, validating that the feelings they have are real and legitimate helps the person process what they feel, provides relief, and encourages expression.

To be accompanied

Emotions are best supported within a safe, nonjudgmental relationship that can accompany them. The formation of traumatic material often happens when someone is too alone or under-resourced to process what they feel. The flip side of this is when the presence of an emotionally safe other helps emotions to be seen, felt, and processed. This type of accompaniment can come from a person or from yourself.

To be experienced

Emotions live in the body; therefore, we can't think our way out of an emotion. Instead, we need to allow emotional energy to be experienced in the body so that it can live out its full wave towards completion. This can be through movement, through staying with a sensation with the support of breath, through art and music, through visualizations and fantasy, through journaling, or by various other means.

To be named

Putting words to what we feel helps emotional energy to be seen, understood, and processed. It connects the right hemisphere of our brain, where most of our emotions live, to our left hemisphere, where language lives, creating a "garden of neural connections," as neuroscience educator Sarah Peyton puts it.[114]

Resonance not advice or reassurance

Emotions like verbal and non-verbal resonance that lets them know that they are seen and they make sense. They do not respond well to being "fixed" or reassured, which makes an assumption about them. Instead, resonance practices meet an emotion where it is and offer it company. These can be statements of warmth and understanding "*Oh, that totally makes sense...*" Or it can be physical gestures such as empathetic eyes or a soft face.

The Change Triangle

The Change Triangle is a powerful framework for understanding and working with emotions. It brings structure to what can often feel amorphous or overwhelming, helping us name what we're feeling and understand why it's there. At any moment, this map can help us pause and ask: *what am I actually feeling? What might be underneath this reaction? What's asking for attention?*

Originally developed by psychologist David Malan and refined by Dr. Diana Fosha (founder of AEDP), the Change Triangle was adapted into its current form by psychotherapist and educator Hilary Jacobs Hendel, whose book *It's Not Always Depression* brings the framework to life with warmth and clarity.[115] It is the clearest and most grounding explanation of emotions I have found. I trained in Hendel's Emotions Education 101 curriculum and draw on it throughout this book as a foundational reference for how we approach emotional processing in collective healing.[116]

At its core, the Change Triangle breaks emotional experience into three categories:

» Core Emotions
» Inhibitory Emotions
» Defenses

Understanding the difference between these categories can help us more clearly identify what we're feeling in any given moment, and begin to work with it rather than being overwhelmed or shut down by it. You can think of the Change Triangle as a kind of emotional compass—a tool that can help you name your state and guide your next step.

The Change Triangle®

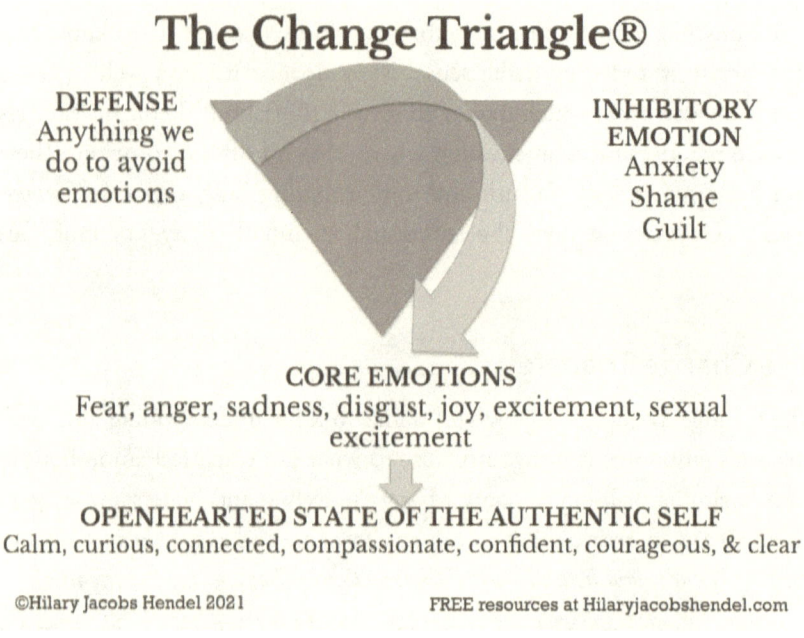

DEFENSE
Anything we
do to avoid
emotions

**INHIBITORY
EMOTION**
Anxiety
Shame
Guilt

CORE EMOTIONS
Fear, anger, sadness, disgust, joy, excitement, sexual
excitement

OPENHEARTED STATE OF THE AUTHENTIC SELF
Calm, curious, connected, compassionate, confident, courageous, & clear

©Hilary Jacobs Hendel 2021   FREE resources at Hilaryjacobshendel.com

Below is a brief overview of each part of the Change Triangle:

Core Emotions (bottom of the triangle)

Core emotions are the bread and butter of our emotional world. These include fear, anger, sadness, disgust, joy, excitement, and sexual excitement. They're hardwired into us from birth, arising automatically in response to specific triggers. They're designed to help us survive and thrive—each with its own intelligence, and each pointing us toward what we need.

When we are able to stay present with core emotions—viscerally, not just intellectually—they tend to move and resolve things. They offer clarity, relief, and a return to connection. However, when they are blocked, avoided, or suppressed, we may find ourselves stuck in other emotional states that feel less clear and more disorienting.

Inhibitory Emotions (top right corner of the triangle)

Inhibitory emotions—shame, guilt, and anxiety—are emotions that come in to suppress core emotions. Their function is to keep us in relationship with others—our families, caregivers, or broader society—by limiting emotional expressions that might threaten belonging or safety.

In small doses, inhibitory emotions can be adaptive. They help us regulate. Guilt can support pro-social behavior. Shame can help us keep it together, just before we go onstage. Anxiety can keep us alert when we're in a high-stakes situation. However, when these emotions are internalized or over-relied on, they can become toxic and disconnect us from our true selves.

Defenses (top left corner of the triangle)

When core emotions or inhibitory emotions feel too threatening to experience—consciously or unconsciously—we reach for defenses. Defenses are strategies we develop to protect ourselves from pain. They can be momentary, like sarcasm or distraction, or deeply embedded, like perfectionism, dissociation, substance use, or emotional withdrawal.

Defenses are not bad. In fact, they're often brilliant. They emerge in childhood or trauma to help us survive, and many have served us well. The goal in working with defenses is not to eliminate them, but to bring them into awareness so we can choose when and how we use them.

Learn more about the Change Triangle by exploring Hilary Jacobs Hendel's book *It's Not Always Depression* or visiting her website at <u>hilaryjacobshendel.com</u>.

LEARN MORE

Thank you for choosing to read this book. If you'd like to stay connected, you can do so through my work at We Heal For All—live Circles, courses & tools, meditations. Subscribe to my Substack for essays and podcast episodes. Learn to facilitate healing-centered groups through my Circle training. Book me for your next team workshop or speaking event.

Website: www.wehealforall.com

Substack: wehealforall.substack.com

Instagram: @we_heal_for_all

Facebook: @wehealforal

ABOUT THE AUTHOR

Feeler by nature, changemaker by trade. Liz Moyer Benferhat, MPA-DP has worked in the sustainable development field for almost 20 years, so she knows how much heart goes into caring about the world. This is why she launched We Heal For All in 2018—to offer language and tools for the inner dimension of this work and bring more healing-centered approaches into the mix. She has a Masters of Public Administration in Development Practice from Columbia University's School of International and Public Affairs. She lives in the Bronx, NY, with her husband and daughter.

ACKNOWLEDGEMENTS
AND GRATITUDE

Anees, my husband, editor, co-captain, champion, creative partner. True co-parent to the development of this book. You are more than my rock. You're the larger ecosystem all of this has taken shape within. I love you.

My family—my mom, sister, cousin—and friends and loved ones who have cheered me on, lifted me up, and spiritually held this project as it came into form.

All of the editors and book development support I received from: Hugh Barker, Sarmad Wali Kahn (you were instrumental, Sarmad!), Dane Cobain, Jamie Jordan, Andrew Weiner, Brianna McCabe, and George Verongos. Thank you for working with me on this, especially those of you who were part of the messier stages of this work.

Early readers and beta readers: Michael Stern, Bruce Nayowith, Kahini Calcuttawalla, Tuğçe Sutas. Your feedback was priceless! It greatly shaped what this book has become.

Publication and launch support: Cori Rupe. Cover design: Kam Bains. Interior design: Linsey Dodaro. Thank you all so much for bringing this vision to life.

Everyone quoted in this book. All of the community members, Circle participants, and collaborators who have been co-building this work with me.

Friends, family, and community members who donated to this project: Laura Araminta, Thouria Benferhat, Kumar Biswas, Alyssa Choudhury, Andrew Carmona, Janet Callahan, Amy Sands, Joanne Fishburn, Jenn Frank, Lori Everest, Shawna Emerick, Emily Holmes, Kyle Konopka, Margaret Kuskin, KateLyn Moyer, James Moyer, Kyle Murphy, Mark Orrs, Nicole Patrick, Andrew Rose, Amy Sands, Arakel Torosian, and Rhoda Vanderhart. I received so much from your support—financially, yes. But even more, energetically and spiritually.

The teachers, mentors, and communities of practice I am blessed to be in relationship with—informed and inspired by. Duane Elgin, a source of inspiration and support in my early years of writing.

My spiritual sister, Kitty Mitchell.

ENDNOTES

CHAPTER 3

1   Parker, K., & Igielnik, R. (2020, May 14). On the cusp of adulthood and facing an uncertain future: What we know about Gen Z so far. Pew Research Center. https://tinyurl.com/pewre-port-genz2020

2   American Psychological Association. (2023, November). Stress in America™ 2023: A nation grappling with psychological impacts of collective trauma. Retrieved from https://www.apa.org/news/press/releases/2023/11/psychological-impacts-collective-trauma

3   Weller, F. (2023). Foreword. In D. Christian, Choosing Earth: Humanity's journey of initiation through breakdown and collapse to a mature planetary civilization (p. 12). New Society Publishers. https://choosingearth.org/wp-content/uploads/2024/05/CE2023_FreePDF_24-04-30.pdf

4   Jones, J. M. (2023, May 30). U.S. mood remains glum; 18% satisfied with state of nation. Gallup News. https://news.gallup.com/poll/1669/general-mood-country.aspx

5   American Psychological Association. (2022, March 10). Stress in America: On second COVID19 anniversary, money, inflation, war pile on to nation stuck in survival mode. American Psychological Association. https://www.apa.org/news/press/releases/stress/2022/march-2022-survival-mode/

6   Roser, M. (2016, December 14; updated February 2024). The short history of global living conditions and why it matters that we know it. Our World in Data. Global Change Data Lab. https://ourworldindata.org/a-history-of-global-living-conditions/

7   Mounk, Y. (2022, October 20). Why political violence is rising in America—and what we can do about it. Brookings Institution. https://www.brookings.edu/articles/why-political-violence-is-rising-in-america-and-what-we-can-do-about-it/

8   Vision of Humanity. (2020, December 30). Global peacefulness falls for the fourth time in the last five years. Institute for Economics & Peace. https://www.visionofhumanity.org/global-peacefulness-falls-for-the-fourth-time-in-the-last-five-years/

9   UC Davis Health. (2022, July 20). Survey finds alarming trend toward political violence. https://health.ucdavis.edu/news/headlines/survey-finds-alarming-trend-toward-political-violence/2022/07

10 Vision of Humanity. (2020, December 30). Global peacefulness falls for the fourth time in the last five years. Institute for Economics & Peace. https://www.visionofhumanity.org/global-peacefulness-falls-for-the-fourth-time-in-the-last-five-years/

11 Kallehauge, K. (2021, June 28). The Global Peace Index 2021 reveals a year of civil unrest. Vision of Humanity. https://www.visionofhumanity.org/global-peace-index-2021-a-year-of-civil-unrest/

12 Pew Research Center. (2020, November 13). America is exceptional in the nature of its political divide. Pew Research Center. https://www.pewresearch.org/shortreads/2020/11/13/america-is-exceptional-in-the-nature-of-its-political-divide/

13 Pew Research Center. (2014, June 12). Political polarization in the American public. Pew Research Center. https://www.pewresearch.org/politics/2014/06/12/political-polarization-in-the-american-public/

14 Pew Research Center. (2022, August 9). As partisan hostility grows, signs of frustration with the two-party system. Pew Research Center. https://www.pewresearch.org/politics/2022/08/09/as-partisan-hostility-grows-signs-of-frustration-with-the-two-party-system/

15 Public Religion Research Institute & The Atlantic. (2019). Ten striking findings on diversity, identity, polarization and inclusion from the 2019 PRRI–Atlantic Survey. Public Religion Research Institute. https://www.prri.org/spotlight/ten-notable-findings-in-2019/

16 Trust for America's Health. (2023, May 24). Pain in the Nation 2023: U.S. death rate due to alcohol, drugs, and suicide increased by 11 percent in 2021. https://www.tfah.org/report-details/pain-in-the-nation-2023/

17 Trust for America's Health. (2023, May 24). Pain in the Nation 2023: U.S. death rate due to alcohol, drugs, and suicide increased by 11 percent in 2021. https://www.tfah.org/report-details/pain-in-the-nation-2023/

18 Clary, A. (2022, January 12). Poll: More Americans are worried than hopeful heading into 2022. APM Research Lab. https://www.apmresearchlab.org/motn/hope-worry-2022

19 Pew Research Center. (2023, April 24). Americans take a dim view of the nation's future, look more positively at the past. Pew Research Center. https://www.pewresearch.org/short-reads/2023/04/24/americans-take-a-dim-view-of-the-nations-future-look-more-positively-at-the-past/

20 Pew Research Center. (2023, October 25). How Americans view future harms from climate change in their community and around the U.S. Pew Research Center. https://www.pewresearch.org/science/2023/10/25/how-americans-view-future-harms-from-climate-change-in-their-community-and-around-the-u-s/

21 Banking Exchange. (2025, May 9). Nearly a third of Americans are pessimistic about their future financial situation. Banking Exchange. https://www.bankingexchange.com/news-feed/item/10311-nearly-a-third-of-americans-are-pessimistic-about-their-future-financial-situation

22 UNICEF. (2024, June). In pursuit of happiness: Girls' striking optimism in a time of crisis. UNICEF. https://data.unicef.org/resources/in-pursuit-of-happiness-girls-striking-optimism-in-a-time-of-crisis/

23 Pew Research Center. (2025, January 16). Emotional well-being. Pew Research Center. https://www.pewresearch.org/2025/01/16/emotional-well-being/

24 Our World in Data. Collective pessimism and our inability to guess the happiness of others. Our World in Data. https://ourworldindata.org/collective-pessimism-and-our-inability-to-guess-the-happiness-of-others

25 Pihkala, P. (2020). Anxiety and the ecological crisis: An analysis of ecoanxiety and climate anxiety. Sustainability, 12(19), 7836. https://doi.org/10.3390/su12197836

26 Turchin, P. (2023). End times: Elites, counterelites, and the path of political disintegration. Penguin Random House.

27 Turchin, P. (2023). End times: Elites, counterelites, and the path of political disintegration. Penguin Random House.

28 Frank, L. K. (1944). What is social order? American Journal of Sociology, 49(5), 470–484. https://doi.org/10.1086/219471

29 Pihkala, P. (2020). Anxiety and the ecological crisis: An analysis of ecoanxiety and climate anxiety. Sustainability, 12(19), 7836. https://doi.org/10.3390/su12197836

30 Durkheim, É. (1893). The division of labour in society. Free Press (trans. Simpson & Taylor).

31 Durkheim, É. (1893). The division of labour in society (p. 129). Free Press (trans. Simpson & Taylor).

32 Wilber, K. (2000). A Theory of Everything: An Integral Vision for Business, Politics, Science, and Spirituality (p. 1). Shambhala Publications.

33 Ritchie, H., OrtizOspina, E., & Roser, M. (2023). Internet [Data page]. Our World in Data. https://ourworldindata.org/internet

34 One of the key indicators for measuring global poverty is the poverty line: the percentage of people throughout the world who live below USD $2.15 per day.

35 Newberg, A., & Waldman, M. R. (2016). How enlightenment changes your brain: The new science of transformation. Avery.

36 Brock, R. N. (2019). [Lecture on trauma and moral foundations]. Unpublished lecture recording. Retrieved from https://tinyurl.com/BrockLecture2019

37 Nin, A. (1961). Seduction of the Minotaur (p. 124). Swallow Press.

CHAPTER 4

38 Brown, A. M. (2019). Pleasure activism: The politics of feeling good. AK Press.

39 Hall, M. P. (1928). The secret teachings of all ages. H.S. Crocker Company. Retrieved from https://tinyurl.com/SecretTeachingsAllAges

40 Briggs, A., & Burke, P. (2002). A Social History of the Media: From Gutenberg to the Internet (2nd ed.). Polity Press

41 Blake, W. (attributed). (n.d.). A culture is a totality of imaginative power. (Citation based on secondary source).

42 Nittle, N. K. (2025, February 13). How BlackRun Newspapers Bolstered the Abolitionist Movement. History.com.

43 Charlton, H. (1989). Saints Alive (Golden Quest Series, Vol. III) (p. 68). Golden Quest.

44 NASA. (2024). How do we know climate change is real? NASA Climate Change: Vital Signs of the Planet. https://science.nasa.gov/climate-change/evidence/

45 Woodbury, Z. (2019). Climate Trauma: Toward a new taxonomy of trauma [Advance publication]. Ecopsychology, 11(1). https://doi.org/10.1089/eco.2018.002

46 Wilber, K. (2017). The religion of tomorrow: A vision for the future of the great traditions—More inclusive, more comprehensive, more complete (p. 210). Shambhala Publications.

47 From a 16th-century poem by Spanish mystic St. John of the Cross, the "dark night of the soul" describes a spiritual seeker wandering alone through their darkest inner terrain—scared, desolate, lost. It's that inevitable point where connection to the Divine feels severed, where despair replaces faith. Yet this devastation is considered essential to spiritual growth, a turning point that precedes breakthrough and transformation.

48 Elgin, D. (2018). Humanity's Great Transition (p. 4). Awakening Earth Project. https://duaneelgin.com/wp-content/uploads/2018/12/HUMANITYS-GREAT-TRANSITION-2.5.pdf

49 This question is fraught with issues, no doubt. Who exactly am I thinking of when I say "past generations?" The elites? Farmers? Depending on class, background, and other forms of status this question can be answered differently, but hopefully my point still lands.

50 Collective Trauma Summit. (2019). Collective trauma and intergenerational healing (p. 4).

    Unpublished manuscript. Retrieved from https://tinyurl.com/CollectiveTraumaSummit2019

51 Peyton, S. (2020, November 11). 10 key concepts of resonant healing. Sarah Peyton. https://sarahpeyton.com/10-key-concepts-of-resonant-healing/

52 Roser, M., & Ritchie, H. (2018). Optimism and pessimism. Our World in Data. https://ourworldindata.org/optimism-and-pessimism

53 Roser, M. (2021). Extreme poverty in brief. Our World in Data. https://ourworldindata.org/extreme-poverty-in-brief

54 Brave Heart, M. Y. H. (2003). The historical trauma response among natives and its relationship with substance abuse: A Lakota illustration. Journal of Psychoactive Drugs, 35(1), 7–13. https://doi.org/10.1080/02791072.2003.10399988

55 Tedeschi, R. G., & Calhoun, L. G. (2004). Posttraumatic growth: Conceptual foundations and empirical evidence. Psychological Inquiry, 15(1), 1–18. https://doi.org/10.1207/S15327965PLI1501_01

56 Mitchell, S. (2018). Sacred instructions: Indigenous wisdom for living spirit-based change. North Atlantic Books.

57 Core emotions are the bread and butter of our emotional world. These include fear, anger, sadness, disgust, joy, excitement, and sexual excitement. They're hardwired into us from birth, arising automatically in response to specific triggers, designed to help us survive and thrive. See Appendix E. for more information.

58 Jacobs Hendel, H. (2018). It's not always depression: Working the change triangle to listen to the body, discover core emotions, and connect to your authentic self. Random House.

CHAPTER 5

59   Hübl, T., & Avritt, J. (2020). Healing collective trauma: A process for integrating our inter-generational and cultural wounds (p. 135). Sounds True. https://www.collectivetraumabook.com/
60   Fosha, D., Siegel, D. J., & Solomon, M. (Eds.). (2009). The healing power of emotion: Affective neuroscience, development, and clinical practice. W. W. Norton & Company.
61   United Nations Sustainable Development Group. (2023, January). The RC leadership profile. https://unsdg.un.org/sites/default/files/2023-01/RC%20Leadership%20Profile_0.pdf

CHAPTER 6

62   Macy, J. (2020, March 7). What's one thing you love about being alive on planet Earth these days? Deep Times Journal. Retrieved from https://journal.workthatreconnects.org/
63   Scharmer, O., & Pomeroy, E. (2024). Fourth person: The knowing of the field. Journal of Awareness-Based Systems Change, 4(1), 19–48. https://doi.org/10.47061/jasc.v4i1.7909

CHAPTER 7

64   Hendel, H. J. (2018). It's not always depression: Working the change triangle to listen to the body, discover core emotions, and connect to your authentic self. Random House.
65   Hendel, H. J. (2018). It's not always depression: Working the change triangle to listen to the body, discover core emotions, and connect to your authentic self. Random House.
66   Fosha, D. (Ed.). (2021). Undoing aloneness and the transformation of suffering into flourishing: AEDP 2.0. American Psychological Association.
67   Peyton, S. (2017). Your resonant self: Guided meditations and exercises to engage your brain's capacity for healing. W. W. Norton & Company.
68   van der Kolk, B. (2014). The body keeps the score: Brain, mind, and body in the healing of trauma. Viking.

CHAPTER 8

69   Meade, M. J. (2025). The hidden unity of life [Audio podcast episode]. In Living Myth. Mosaic Multicultural Foundation. https://www.mosaicvoices.org/episode-134-the-hidden-unity-of-life
70   Jacobs Hendel, H. (2018). It's not always depression: Working the Change Triangle to listen to the body, discover core emotions, and connect to your authentic self. Random House.
71   Rosenberg, M. B. (2015). Nonviolent communication: A language of life (3rd ed.). PuddleDancer Press.
72   Hayes, S. C., Strosahl, K. D., & Wilson, K. G. (2012). Acceptance and commitment therapy: The process and practice of mindful change (2nd ed.). Guilford Press.
73   Rilke, R. M. (2001). Letters to a young poet (M. D. Herter Norton, Trans.). W. W. Norton & Company. (Original work published 1934)
74   Scharmer, O. (2023, May 18). Personal communication, Presencing Institute Core Team Strategy Meeting, Berlin, Germany.
75   Marsh, A. A. (2018). The neuroscience of empathy: Cognitive and affective components and their neural bases. Current Opinion in Behavioral Sciences, 19, 110–115. https://doi.org/10.1016/j.cobeha.2017.12.016

CHAPTER 9

76   Fosha, D. (2000). Meta-therapeutic processes and the affects of transformation: Affirmation and the healing affects. Derner Institute for Advanced Psychological Studies, Adelphi University. https://test.aedpinstitute.org/wp-content/uploads/2015/06/Fosha_Meta_Therapeutic_Processes_2000.pdf

77   Possibility Management. (n.d.). Vera Luísa Franco. Retrieved August 5, 2025, from https://possibilitymanagement.org/vera-franco

78   Fosha, D. (Ed.). (2021). Undoing aloneness and the transformation of suffering into flourishing: AEDP 2.0. American Psychological Association.

CHAPTER 11

79   Brock, R. N. (2019). [Lecture on trauma and moral foundations]. Unpublished lecture recording. Retrieved from https://tinyurl.com/BrockLecture2019

80   Durkheim, É. (1893). The division of labour in society (p. 129). Free Press (trans. Simpson & Taylor).

81   Schwartz, R. C. (2021). No bad parts: Healing trauma and restoring wholeness with the Internal Family Systems model. Sounds True.

82   Jung, C. G. (1969). The archetypes and the collective unconscious (2nd ed., R. F. C. Hull, Trans.). Princeton University Press.

83   Family Constellations is a therapeutic approach developed by Bert Hellinger. It is based on the idea that unresolved pain or trauma within a family system can be carried by descendants and manifest in their lives--a great grandparent that was exiled from the family, for instance, or a distant relative who died too early and was never properly grieved. The method uses group processes to make these dynamics visible and offer healing at the soul level of the family system and ripple out to affect the health and well-being of individual family members.

84   In his book The Tears of the Ancestors, Daan van Kampenhout introduces us to the term 'tribal soul' to describe a soul layer that exists somewhere in between the family soul and the "greater soul," a term Bert Hellinger, founder of Family Constellations, uses to describe the collective field that all of humanity is part of.
          The tribal soul doesn't refer to tribes within the anthropological sense, but "any collective that defines itself as different from others." An individual can span and be part of multiple tribal souls, even ones that are in potential conflict with one another. For instance, I as an American am part of the tribal soul of my country. I can sense into my own lived experience and find this. When I say, "I am an American," a particular set of feelings, images, and impressions arise for me that are part of my identity, history and sense of self.

85   Van Kampenhout, D. (2008). The tears of the ancestors: Victims and perpetrators in the tribal soul. Lotus/Light Publishing.

86   Full quote: "…what I am experiencing is a part of my being that is not located within my individual soul, or within the family familiar regions of my personality. I have touched a place where reason and logic are bypassed. In a realm of the soul, which is wider, more spacious than what I have experienced before. I am experiencing the tribal soul. And although it may be true that I have an individual soul, it is equally true that the tribal soul has me."

87   Many indigenous cultures and shamanic traditions view communities as having a soul, and believe that it is vital and necessary to heal and do spiritual work at this level. Both Kampenhout and Hellinger offer us systemic modalities we can use to work at the collective field level. The "collective field" can be thought of as a tapestry or quilt of energy that exists among and between a group of people. Ken Wilber's Integral Theory offers us the term "we-space:" The idea is that between two individuals there is a third presence that exists outside of both of them. For instance, if you and I are sitting together in a room, there is you, there is me, and there is a third "we-space" that exists between us. This third space is the field of energy between us and is something we can sense into, build a relationship with, and work with together. Each tribal soul has its own history and set of experiences that shape the collective wounds held within it. As individuals, we can practice forming a relationship with the tribal souls we are part of, and the collective wounds that live in each and manifest in our own liveswhat type of religious

persecution, for instance, did my ancestors experience that might help explain the existential fear I feel in response to the threat of cancel culture? In what ways can I work at the spiritual level of things to help those parts of the tribal soul within me heal and find their proper place within the greater web of sacred, unconditional love?

88   Porges, S. W. (2011). The polyvagal theory: Neurophysiological foundations of emotions, attachment, communication, and self regulation. W. W. Norton.

89   Menakem, R. (2017). My grandmother's hands: Racialized trauma and the pathway to mending our hearts and bodies. Central Recovery Press.

90   Van Kampenhout, D. (2008). The tears of the ancestors: Victims and perpetrators in the tribal soul (p. 11). Lotus/Light Publishing.

91   Maslow, A. H. (1943). A theory of human motivation. Psychological Review, 50(4), 370–396. https://doi.org/10.1037/h0054346

92   Marker, S. (2003, August). Unmet human needs. In G. Burgess & H. Burgess (Eds.), Beyond Intractability. Conflict Information Consortium, University of Colorado. Retrieved from https://www.beyondintractability.org/essay/human_needs

93   Identity, in this context, extends beyond an internal psychological sense of self, and is instead understood to be shaped through one's relationship with the external world. It becomes a source of conflict when it is dismissed, devalued, or threatened—particularly by groups with differing identities or systems that fail to recognize its legitimacy.

94   Through her work, she has found that this trait can be found in over 100 species in nature, if not more. These people's (or cats' or fruit flies'…) brains work a little differently. Their brains process information more deeply, which leads them to have a heightened awareness of things; to see things below the surface. They ultimately take in and notice more, which makes them more prone to feeling overwhelmed, due to intense or chaotic stimuli.

95   Aron, E. N. (2020). The highly sensitive person: How to thrive when the world overwhelms you (25th anniversary ed.). Citadel Press.

96   Akomolafe, B. (2023, April 7). The Revolution Will Not Be Psychologized, Part 2 [Audio podcast episode]. In The Emerald. Buzzsprout. (Min. 37:30)

Appendix

97   Cultural Survival. (2021, March 2). A bridge between worlds in Siberia: Tatyana Vassilievna Kobezhikova. Cultural Survival Quarterly. Retrieved from https://www.culturalsurvival.org/publications/cultural-survival-quarterly/bridge-between-worlds-siberia-tatyana-vassilievna

98   KahnJohn, M. (Diné), & Koithan, M. (2015). Living in health, harmony, and beauty: The Diné (Navajo) hózhó wellness philosophy. Global Advances in Health and Medicine, 4(3), 24–30. Retrieved from https://www.ncbi.nlm.nih.gov/articles/PMC4424938/

99   Zen Peacemakers International. (n.d.). AuschwitzBirkenau: Bearing Witness Retreat [Web page]. Retrieved from https://tinyurl.com/BearingWitnessRetreat

100   van Kampenhout, D. (n.d.). Systemic Ritual and the Four Directions: blending family constellations with shamanic ritual [Web page]. Retrieved from https://tinyurl.com/SystemicRitualKampenhout

101   Macy, J., & Brown, M. Y. (2014). Coming back to life: The updated guide to the Work That Reconnects. New Society Publishers.

102   Hübl, T., & Sasportas, Y. (2016). The Pocket Project: Collective Trauma Integration initiative and approach [Web page]. Retrieved from https://pocketproject.org/ pocketproject.org+13secondrenaissance.net+13pocketproject.org+13

103   Haines, S. K. (n.d.). Somatics for transformative justice and embodied leadership [Web page]. Retrieved from https://www.stacihaines.com/about

104   Baldwin, L. V. (2003). The legacy of Martin Luther King, Jr.: The boundaries of law, politics, and religion. University of Notre Dame Press.

105   Gould, D. B. (2009). Moving politics: Emotion and ACT UP's fight against AIDS. University of Chicago Press.

106   Kindred Southern Healing Justice Collective. (2006). Healing justice framework: Collective healing and social transformation [Web page]. Retrieved from https://kindredsouthernhjcol-

lective.org/

107   Brave Heart, M. Y. H. (2003). The historical trauma response among Natives and its relation-ship with substance abuse: A Lakota illustration. Journal of Psychoactive Drugs, 35(1), 7–13. https://doi.org/10.1080/02791072.2003.10399988

108   DeGruy, J. (2005). Post traumatic slave syndrome: America's legacy of enduring injury and healing. Joy DeGruy Publications.

109   Menakem, R. (2017). My grandmother's hands: Racialized trauma and the pathway to mend-ing our hearts and bodies. Central Recovery Press.

110   Climate Psychology Alliance. (n.d.). Climate psychology alliance. Retrieved from https://www.

climatepsychologyalliance.org/

111   Tutu, D. M. (1999). No future without forgiveness. Doubleday.

112   Clark, P. (2010). The Gacaca courts, postgenocide justice and reconciliation in Rwanda: Justice without lawyers. Cambridge University Press.

113   Zehr, H. (2002). The little book of restorative justice. Good Books.

114   Peyton, S. (2022, March). Resonant Healing Practitioner Training [Personal communication].

115   Hendel, H. J. (2018). It's not always depression: Working the change triangle to listen to the body, discover core emotions, and connect to your authentic self. Random House.

116   Hendel, H. J., & Sanford, H. (n.d.). Emotions Education 101™ [Professional training curricu-lum].

www.ingramcontent.com/pod-product-compliance
Lightning Source LLC
Chambersburg PA
CBHW021617120626
46545CB00001B/272